frontispiece: the coat of arms of the city of Vitry-sur-Orne in France, the source of the name of the author's family

TRIPPING OVER EUROPE
Expert Advice on Making Travel Easy

by
Eugene J. Wittry

Copyright 2001
Eugene J. Wittry

Other Books By the Author
Wittry, Witry, Vitry :A Family History

Published 2001 by

HERITAGE BOOKS, INC.
1540E Pointer Ridge Place, Bowie, Maryland 20716
1-800-398-7709
www.heritagebooks.com

ISBN 0-7884-1850-5

A Complete Catalog Listing Hundreds of Titles
On History, Genealogy, and Americana
Available Free Upon Request

This book is dedicated

to Jack and June Palko,

the best travel companions

we could hope to have.

Contents

Preface .... page xv

1. Why Travel on Your Own?
Because it is fun! .... page 1
The subject of this book 2
Why this book? 3
Structure of the book 4
Tour notes 5
Local eyes 6
Basic preparation 6
Select your destination 6
Select your travel partner(s) 7
Plan, plan, plan 7
Learn a few words 8
Crooked cab driver? 8
Jerry on tours 9

2. Planning the Itinerary
Where to go 11
When to plan 12
What to see and do 13
When to go 13
How long to stay 15
Sources of information 16
Managing time 18
Read, read, read 19
Visas 20
How to spend a rainy day 20
Operating hours 20

Be flexible	21
Special days	21

3. Packing
How much to pack?	23
John's and Margie's drawers	24
What do I need?	24
Lost luggage	25
Clothing	26
The art of packing	27
Grooming	28
Medications	29
Documents	30
It sometimes helps not to speak the language	31
Security wallet	32
Money	33
Genealogy aids	33
Miscellaneous items	34
Where is north?	36
Gifts	36
Packing each container	37

4. Flight Arrangements
We're off!	41
Which airline?	41
Airline to where?	42
Buying the ticket	43
Verify your flights	43
Check-in	44
The bomb in the suitcase	44
Departure gate	45
On the plane	46
No rest for the wicked	47
Customs	48
The two-fisted drinker	49
Jet lag	49

5. Renting a Car
Selecting an agency	51
Crossing borders	52
Selecting a car	52
The advantage of folding mirrors	53
Added features	54
Rental desk	54
Picking up the car	55
Where is M-VI?	56
Leaving the airport	56

6. Driving
Expect the unexpected	59
Right hand drive	59
Reading maps	60
Tollway traps	61
Portuguese conventions	61
Where did you come from?	62
Full service toll booths	62
Speed limits	63
Driving conventions	64
The circus of Paris	66
Traffic lights	66
The power of a U-ey	67
What country are we in?	67
Signs	67
The great chase scene	69
Into and out of town	69
In town	70
Hôtel de l'Ouest	71
Pedestrian rights	72
Parking in the Italian Tijuana	72
Parking	72
Parking lots (car parks in the U.K.)	73
Traffic jam at Orly	74
Fire!	74

Street parking meters	75
Crisis in Sarlat	75
Police	76

7. Public Transportation

Public transportation	79
Trains	79
The Vienna express	81
Trolleys and buses	81
Subways	82
Beware of overconfidence	83
Taxis	83
Why a Japanese story?	84
Boats	85

8. Lodging

Availability	87
A thousand years old	88
Mont St. Michel	89
Selecting a place for the night	89
Nude bather	90
Reservations	90
Bargain basement	91
Timing	92
Which tower is which?	93
Mom and pop hotels	93
The phantom bellhop	94
Bed and breakfast	94
House rental	95
Hotel conventions	96
Which floor is which?	98

9. Food

The ultimate go-no go gauge	101
Hamburger?	101
Breakfast	102
Lunch	103

Dinner	105
Applauding the chef	107
Local specialties	108
Shrimp eyes	109
Liechtenstein meatloaf	109
Tipping	110
Chicken under the menu	110
Dogs	110
Snacks	111

10. Water Closet

I gotta go, but where?	113
Multi-flush	114
Customs	114
Types of toilets	115
Turkish style	116
Collecting flushing devices	117
Where to find one?	117
The two franc shower	118
How to identify one	118
Men versus women	118
Small towns	119
How to find water	119
Emergencies	119

11. The Best Things in Life Are Free

Tourist advice	121
Rudeness	123
Road signs	123
Stop and smell the roses	124
Scenery	124
Topless beaches	124
Cities	125
Flexibility	126
Cemeteries	126
National monuments	127
Music	128

A bargain outing	129
Parks	129
Living statue	130
Second best isn't always bad	131
Tours	131
Stammtisch Willi	131
Senior discounts	132
People	132
The palsied hardware clerk	133

12. Experience Your Roots

Where they lived	135
The landscape	135
The village and city	136
Farming	136
Houses	137
Furnishings	137
Church	138
Ancient roots	138
Food	139
Markets	139
Neighbors	140
Sources	140

13. Family Research

National archives	141
Professional genealogists	142
Heraldry	142
Local registries	142
Parish records	143
Histories and maps	143
Mr. Miny of Nommern	144
Church records	145
Libraries	145
Cemeteries	146
The living are important too	146
Interviews	147

14. Purchases
General rules	149
The lonesome statue	149
Where to shop	150
Art market	152
Memory items	152
Making a purchase	153
Store hours	154
Instant rebate	155
Careful about limits!	155
Who died on the plane?	156
Electronics	156
They cremated my baby	156

15. Handling Money
Forms of money	159
Romin' thieves	161
Exchanging money	161
Currency conventions	163
Coins	163
Purse	164

16. Telephones
Intimidation	167
Finding a public telephone	167
The telephone thief	168
Conventions	168
Paying for the call	169
The telephone curse	169
Important calls to make	170

17. Safety
Hazards	171
Valuables	172
Walking	172
Hotel	173
Car	173

Welcome to Paris	174
Accidents	174

18. Language

Inhibition	175
Pear	176
Language adds seasoning	176
Instant experts	176
Language is not essential	177
Dictionary of terms	177
Gelb	178
The absolute minimum	178
Vocabulary - Basic phrases	179
The lace maker	180
Pocket phrase book	180
Make an investment	181
The perils of English English	181
Vocabulary - Buildings	182
Vocabulary - Calendar	183
Vocabulary - Clothing	184
Vocabulary - Colors	185
Vocabulary - Customs	186
Vocabulary - Directions	187
Vocabulary - Drinks	188
Vocabulary - Family	189
Vocabulary - Foods	190
Vocabulary - Fruit	191
Vocabulary - Genealogy	192
Vocabulary - Jewelry	193
Vocabulary - Lodging	194
Vocabulary - Meals	195
Vocabulary - Meat	196
Vocabulary - Money	197
Vocabulary - Numbers - small	198
Vocabulary - Numbers - large	199
Vocabulary - Shopping	200
Vocabulary - Signs	201

Vocabulary - Time	202
Vocabulary - Transportation	203
Vocabulary - Vegetables	204
Phonics	205
Vocabulary - Phonics - Portuguese	207
Vocabulary - Phonics	208

19. Returning home

Preparation	209
Flight confirmation	209
Packing	210
The pétanque bombs	211
Returning the car	212
Check-in	212
Left luggage	213
Foreign currency	213
The flight	214
Arrival	215
Just one bottle	215
Home at last!	216

20. Do's and Don't's

Introduction	217
Shutdown	217
Looking American	218
Why can't you speak English?	218
Communications	219
The irate Rhine maiden	220
Dogs	220
Solicitations	221
The hurried cab hustler	222
Building conventions	223
Americain flambé	223
Food and drink	224
I refuse	224
That's it	225

Preface

My wife, Nancy, and I have traveled abroad each of the ten years since my retirement. Two trips were to Asia, and nine were to Europe. When I was working for a living, business occasionally took me to various countries in Europe. It brought both Nancy and me into close contact with people from France, Belgium and Switzerland. Since all of these people spoke English fluently, and since we learned to care for them as friends, we set out to learn French. Our French is highly accented and is definitely not colloquial, but it is adequate to give us great satisfaction while traveling in France. It has also given us the confidence to travel in other countries, even though we know little or nothing of the local language. These trips have been very enjoyable and educational.

As I planned my retirement, I began to think about genealogy. At that time I was not so much interested in the subject itself as I was in answering a family question that was about a hundred years old. The maiden name of my paternal grandmother was Wittry, the same as the family name of my grandfather. My grandparents, and of course, their children, used to joke about the possibility that they might be related. Grandpa's parents came to this country from Beidweiler, Luxembourg in 1853. He was born here. Grandma came from Herborn, Luxembourg with her father and siblings in 1880. By coincidence, both families settled in Aurora, Illinois where the two met.

I decided to try to determine whether they were really related. Eventually I answered the question. They were indeed related – second cousins, once removed. By the time I learned this, I had been infected with the genealogy bug. Eventually I traced the family tree back to the 16th century, including the distaff side of each ancestral marriage. This in turn led to an overwhelming desire to visit Luxembourg to see where the family originated. After a number of such visits, I have come to deeply appreciate the value of experiencing first hand the roots of my family. I hope to share some of that with you while encouraging you to travel in Europe and to visit your roots. The rewards of both are great.

Some few years ago we were visiting with old friends, Jack and June Palko. They were enjoyable company and were interested in our travels. Their trips had been limited to countries where English was the native language. Although they did venturesome things such as scuba diving and skiing on both snow and water, they were reluctant to travel in a country where they didn't know the language. As we assured them that this was really not a problem, we found ourselves offering to take them on a self-guided grand tour of France the next summer.

They accepted. Then, on the way home, we asked ourselves what we had done. Could our rather casual friendship survive two or three weeks of very close company? We decided that we would end the trip in one of two ways – as the very closest of friends or as people who never wanted to see one another again. Well, we have now traveled together for five years in a row. We have a great time. If you like the little stories scattered throughout this text, thank Jack and June. They have a delightful talent for seeing the light and bright side of everything. Nancy says that we laugh our way through Europe.

Our first trip was so great that we considered writing a book about it. But, after a few weeks at home, we realized that the story was too personal. It would not be of interest to anyone who did not know the personalities involved. However, after four such trips it dawned on me that we did have something of interest to write about. That is, how to travel like we do. Many people have expressed a desire to do so, but are hesitant. Other people, who do travel on their own, love to tell stories of their travels. Hence this book, with travel advice and with illustrative stories.

I would be remiss if I did not pay credit to those who made the book possible. First of all, thanks to my wife, Nancy, who travels with me all the time, my partner at home and on the road. Then thanks again to Jack and June Palko. Thanks to John and Margie Wagner, to Jerry and Mary Klein, to Ed and April Laughlin, and to Jacques and Michèle Ravanat. All of them contributed stories of their exploits and bits of wisdom to aid travelers. As you will be able to tell from the text, Jacques and Michèle spent about half of one trip with us. Six people were even more fun than four.

A special thanks to Jerry Klein, husband of Mary. He is an experienced traveler by hobby, an outstanding editorialist by profession, and an excellent writer of local history by avocation. His encouragement, editing and inspiration have been a godsend to me. Besides, we very much enjoyed sharing a beer or two as we exchanged war stories and planned this book.

Finally, another special thanks to Jeff Rashid who created the illustrations that illuminate this book. As you can see, he is an excellent artist with a whimsical sense of humor. I know that he has good taste, since he recently married our younger daughter. He also edited this text, finding a number of typos and awkward wordings. A tough job — and greatly appreciated.

None of these people is a genealogist, but all are travelers. The genealogical part of this text is mine. The travel part is ours. I sincerely hope you enjoy both parts and benefit from them.

Chapter 1
Why Travel on Your Own?

Because it is fun!

Fun! Romance! Adventure! And a few misadventures! Travel with a tour group if you are insecure or if you don't have the time or energy to plan your own trip. It is a very practical and comfortable way to travel. But, if you like to strike out on your own, you can have a lot more enjoyment doing things just the way that suits you best. However, and this is a big however, if something goes wrong – and it will – you have no-one to blame but yourself. However again, if you have a sense of humor and are willing to "go with the flow," you can find enjoyment in the things that go wrong. They make for some interesting adventures, as you will see throughout the book.

If you are interested in the roots of your family, you definitely cannot experience them effectively as part of a tour. The tour probably will not go to the places where your family came from. Even if it does, it might not give you free time to explore. Even if it does that, the time will certainly be inadequate. You need to have the flexibility to explore by yourself, to chat with local people, and to flex your itinerary in response to what you learn.

The subject of this book

This book is about how to gain firsthand knowledge about your family roots while traveling independently. The majority of the travel advice relates to Western Europe, which is the origin of most Americans. This book is different from the typical travel guide. It doesn't tell you a lot about all of the places you might visit. It doesn't list hotels and restaurants. It does, however, tell you how to select hotels and restaurants, how to plan an itinerary, how to arrange transportation, and generally, how to obtain the most at the least cost and pain.

Tours take you to major cities and historic sites. They drive you in buses, put you up in first class hotels, and provide you with guides who lecture you at great length about the history and art of the locale. They also feed you set meals. You have little time on your own, and little opportunity to choose options.

Many people, including me, have found tours to be confusing. You pass through many places, so quickly that the images tend to merge together and become blurred. There was an old comedy movie on this subject. The title was *If It's Tuesday, This Must Be Belgium*.

We recommend, however, that you take at least one tour. It will give you a feel of the territory. It will also teach you by experience many of the things that are recommended in this book. Then, when it is over, ask yourself a few questions.

- Did I enjoy myself thoroughly?
- Did I like the meal selections?
- Did I find my companions stimulating, nobody a pest or a chronic complainer?
- Did I find my free time less enjoyable?
- Was I satisfied with the cost?
- Did I find most of the lectures interesting?
- Did I discover wonderful new things?
- Did I satisfy my desire for knowledge about my roots?

If your answers to the above questions are generally affirmative, then you should probably stick with tours. However, if some of your answers are negative, then ask yourself these other questions.

- Do I want to chat with local people?
- Am I curious about life in small villages?

- Do I want to eat more of the local cuisine?
- Do I want to minimize my travel expenses?
- Do I want to be independent?
- Do I want to be able to flex my schedule?
- Do I want to discover new things?
- Am I adventuresome?
- Do I like to do things at my own pace?
- Do I want to see and feel the locale where my family lived?
- Do I want to know more about my family roots?

If your answers to these latter questions are generally affirmative, then read on and enjoy. If not, you might be able to return this book for a refund or give it to a friend.

Why this book?

I had traveled in Europe a number of times for my employer. During those trips I was fortunate in being able to explore the country a bit during my free time. In most of the places that I visited, I had work acquaintances who were kind enough to give me suggestions about where to go and what to see. I thoroughly enjoyed these opportunities, but regretted the fact that I had so little free time to explore.

Just before my retirement I went on a tour of Europe with our older daughter and a choir to which she belonged. We had a very nice time. However, both she and I found ourselves frequently "bugging out" on planned tours so that we could explore by ourselves. Upon returning to the group, we invariably found that we had done more and enjoyed it more than did the rest of the people. I remember one particular time in Paris when we stopped by a small delicatessen to buy some bread, cheese, fruit and wine. We sat on a doorstep by the Seine and had a picnic. I noticed that tourists would stare at us enviously, thinking that those French really know how to enjoy themselves. I also noticed the French looking at us enviously as we enjoyed the food and ambiance.

In addition to enjoying the travel itself, I began to make detours to places where my ancestors had lived. Despite the fact that most birth, marriage and death records are available here in the U.S., I found a wealth of local information that is only available on-site. I have photographed houses where my ancestors lived, and have been in some of them. I have found local publications that describe "the old days." I have seen old local customs that still endure. I have met relatives – and introduced them to one another. I have even arranged a family reunion in "The Old Country." Believe me, there is a great deal of knowledge and emotional satisfaction to be had by traveling independently and using the opportunity to learn more about your family history.

Over the years Nancy and I have been at a number of dinner parties where people talked about their travels. We began to notice that the travelers were of two types. Those who traveled on tours seemed to have nothing more to say than to list the places they had been or to compare the qualities of various tour agencies. Those who traveled on their own had interesting stories to relate about their adventures. When I retired, we agreed that it was now time to do some serious traveling. It was not a difficult decision for us to choose the do-it-yourself route. Besides, we were raised during the Great Depression. We don't spend money on things that we don't need or don't want. My wife is a bookkeeper by avocation. She has calculated that we travel for about 50% of the cost of organized tours.

Our favorite travel companions are Jack and June from Phoenix. They live in a retirement community with many traveling neighbors. When they compare itineraries, they find that their neighbors are amazed at the things that Jack and June have experienced. They think we are all multi-millionaires. These neighbors prefer to travel with tours. They visit the same major cities and tourist sites, but they miss out on the fascinating things that we have seen in out-of-the-way places. For this they envy us. And they should!

Of course, during our travels we have made many mistakes and have learned many tricks of the trade. To plan our trips, I have collected and digested innumerable travel guides. They provide a lot of information, but they do not tell you *how to travel*. That is the purpose of this book. It is intended to share our tricks of the trade and to minimize the mistakes that you make, so you can travel on your own.

Structure of the book

This book is organized into chapters that approach a trip chronologically. It begins with planning, continues with flight arrangements, customs, hotels, etc., and ends with your return home.

Each chapter addresses a single topic in some detail. It contains advice on how to prepare for and enjoy your travel. The text is light in tone, as if an experienced friend of yours is giving you some travel advice. There is no attempt to tell you about specific places or facilities, other than to relate a few of our experiences as illustrations.

To give the text another personal touch, I have included the experiences and adventures of six couples:
- Nancy and Gene (me) from Peoria, Illinois,
- June and Jack from Phoenix, Arizona,
- Margie and John from Peoria, Illinois,
- Mary and Jerry from Germantown, Illinois,
- April and Ed from Port St. Lucie, Florida, and
- Michèle and Jacques from St. Ismier, France.

Each of these couples travels alone and with other couples. Each couple has its own style, and each has added to the practical advice and humorous experiences in this book. Of course, I am very grateful to them for sharing their experiences with me – and with you.

Tour notes

A story from Jerry will illustrate what I was saying earlier in this chapter about the inherent limitations of tours. Jerry and I were exchanging tales of adventure over a stein of German beer one day. The conversation moved to the pros and cons of tours. He related three personal experiences that illustrate some of the limitations of tours.

He overheard some people discussing the tours they had taken. One said, "We did Norway in a week." How much appreciation of Norway did those people gain? Think of Oslo, the fjords, the Lapplanders, the mountains, Viking history. One could spend many weeks in Norway.

Jerry was on one tour that included a visit to the Louvre museum in Paris. This is well renowned as the best and largest art museum in the world. The tour director allowed Jerry's group one whole hour to "do the Louvre." He wisely declined.

Jerry is a kindly and gentle man. Yet, he told me a final story that illustrates how frustrating unpleasant companions can be. On the same tour, a woman complained loudly and constantly. She got on his nerves beyond his capacity for tolerance. As they left the bus upon their return home, he was following her. She complained one last time — and he kicked at her! He missed.

Local eyes

Our younger daughter has traveled extensively, both on business and for pleasure. She has worked for a year in Tokyo and in London. If we doubted the benefits of traveling on our own, one of her observations would have settled any concerns. Our favorite country in Europe is France. We go there rather often. Our daughter commented that, "You see France like a Frenchman." We treasure that thought.

May you see France like a Frenchman, Germany like a German, Spain like a Spaniard. May you experience what your ancestors experienced. If you do, then we will know that this book has been worthwhile.

Basic preparation

To give you a better feel for the organization of the book, let's take a bit of time here to start preparation for a trip. The rest of this chapter is organized in somewhat the same fashion as the rest of the book.

Select your destination

The first thing for you to do is to decide where you want to go. If the language of the country where one of your ancestors came from is a concern (it need not be as much of a concern as you think,) then you might want to make your first independent trip to England, or Scotland or Ireland or Wales. The problem with those places however, is that you have to drive on the wrong side of the road. That is not an insoluble problem either, but it makes for some interesting experiences.

If you are worried about both language and driving conventions, then you might select the Netherlands as your target of choice. They drive on the right side of the road, and the percentage of the population that speaks English is about the same as in Los Angeles. Another good alternative is Portugal. It is a beautiful country with lots of history. Most of the young people speak English well, since an English language television station is very popular there.

Be sure to select a destination that has a culture which interests you. You can find a lot of natural beauty in France, ancient history in

Italy, flowers in the Netherlands, bargains in Spain and Portugal, arts in England, beer in Germany, music in Austria. Of course, you can experience your family roots in the country or countries from which your family emigrated. Name your own poison. Maybe I shouldn't have said that.

Select your travel partner(s)

Your travel partner or partners should be selected with care. One of you should be able to read maps. One of you should be good at arithmetic for calculating rates of exchange. You should generally have the same interests and similar energy levels. At the very least, your companions should be tolerant of the time you spend exploring your roots. You could go it totally alone, but I would not recommend that. You would have nobody to share your adventures with, and you would have nobody to blame when things go wrong.

Seriously, shared travel is the most fun. In addition, it is nice to have a few minds at work when there is a problem to be solved. Limit the size of the group to no less than two people and no more than four. The reason for the lower limit is stated above. The reason for the upper limit is that European cars don't handle more than four people comfortably. More on that in a later chapter.

Plan, plan, plan

I have never heard of a successful military campaign that wasn't well planned. On the other hand, I must admit that some well-planned military campaigns were total failures. Travel is easier to plan than a military campaign. There is no obvious enemy trying to undo your plans, unless you consider Murphy's law to be an enemy.

Buy or borrow as much travel literature as you can. Your local lending library is a good place to start. Book shops are full of travel literature. Most countries maintain an embassy or a consulate in major U.S. cities. These offices usually have literature that they make available at no charge. Travel guidebooks often list the addresses of consulates and foreign tourist offices where literature can be obtained by mail. I'd suggest that you obtain two copies of this literature. Obtain the first a year in advance so that you can begin active planning. Obtain the second in the spring of the year in which you travel. The information and prices will be current.

Chapter 2 contains more detailed information on planning an itinerary. It includes planning for your on-site genealogical research, if that is your bag.

Learn a few words

Learn a few words in the language of the country or countries to which you plan to travel. Most people are complimented if a visitor at least tries to speak a few words of the local language. I have heard many people complain about hostile treatment in Paris. I have never heard of anyone being badly treated in Paris if he had just a minimal French vocabulary – and used it. We have found most people in each country to be friendly and helpful. We do run into an occasional grouch. You can even do that in New York.

If you intend to talk to local people to learn more about your family, the use of a few words of the language of the country will go far to break the ice. The other person is likely to have an adequate command of English. Besides, sign language goes a long way, especially if the other person has taken a liking to you because of your interest in his country and language. One of the most rewarding things is listening to someone talk about local history – from the resident's point of view. It is far more interesting than what is written in history books.

A later chapter of this book gives a limited vocabulary of words and expressions that you might find practical. These words and expressions are in English. I leave it to you to look up the translations. It will be your investment in the target language.

Crooked cab driver?

Here is a short, true story that will illustrate the value of having – and using – a rudimentary vocabulary in the local language.

Nancy and I were on our first visit to Paris. We had only one day to enjoy some of the sights, and then had to go to the airport to fly to Geneva, Switzerland. We picked up a cab to take us to the air terminal, which is located near the Arch of Triumph. The air terminal is a convenient central location where you can check in for your flight. You check your luggage, board a bus, and worry about nothing as you are driven to the airport.

Nancy felt courageous about her then very limited French, because she was talking to the back of the cab driver. They began to have a lively conversation. The next thing I knew, we were on the expressway, heading for the airport. I called to the driver and reminded him that he was to take us to the air terminal. He turned around with prolific apologies. Was he a crook who was hoping to get us to pay a large fare? I seriously doubt it. He tried to refuse payment. Since he and Nancy had a great time, and since she had a good practical French lesson, I was pleased to pay for a bit of extra riding.

Jerry on tours

Jerry offered the following thoughts on why he prefers to avoid tours as a method of travel. As you might be able to tell from the text, Jerry is an accomplished professional writer.

"One of the great advantages of traveling on your own, as this book so strongly recommends, is that you can be flexible. If you like a place, stay. If you don't, leave. You aren't condemned to suffer a locale you might find intolerable, or to miss the opportunity to linger at some place that you might find particularly attractive.

"On a tour, with all its security, you are forever at the mercy of the omnipotent schedule. Bags packed and on the bus by 8:00 a.m. Lunch at noon. Ten minutes to go to the bathroom. Back on the bus. And off tomorrow to some place that some other person has selected for you.

"There we were in the summer of 1989 in our rented Fiat, with a Sunday in Salzburg before heading to Munich for a few days, and then flying home. Accommodations in and around Salzburg were impossible. Too full. Too expensive. In desperation, we drove into the countryside and found – finally – small flag at the end of a lane with the words 'Zimmer frei' – room available.

"It was a spanking new chalet, the fields with ginger-colored cows, the balconies flaming with geraniums. And virtually no-one was there. We looked at a room, three floors up, a balcony with table and chairs, shower in the room, the toilet across the hall. For $11 each, breakfast included. And this 'frühstück' consisted of coffee and milk, ham, cheese, bread, and home-made preserves.

"We stayed for three days. You can do that when you are on your own. The view from our room was of rolling green hills across which (it seemed) Julie Andrews would appear momentarily with the Von Trapp children in tow. We wandered through the storybook villages and lakes of the Salzkammergut – Fuschlsee, St. Gilgen, Hallstatt – and thoroughly enjoyed our unscheduled 3-day stop in the middle of what some might call nowhere. It became one of our most cherished travel memories, simply because we were able to be more flexible. Munich will have to await another trip."

Chapter 2
Planning the Itinerary

Where to go

Your first challenge is to decide where you want to go. As I said in Chapter 1, you might want to pick your first country (or countries) based upon your limited language skills and/or concern for what side of the road people drive on. You might have a specific country that is of particular interest to you because your ancestors came from there. I have noticed over the years that it is a rare Irishman who doesn't want to pay a visit to the "Auld Sod." Whatever you decide, limit your itinerary to one particular country. Tours have demonstrated over the years that people who spend one to three days in each of a number of countries become confused. When they arrive home they can't remember what they experienced or where they experienced it. Maybe that is why Jerry's acquaintances said that they "did Norway in a week."

Now that I have cautioned you to limit yourself to one country, I'll admit that we don't always do that. Nancy and I frequently make a quick side trip across the border from the country that is our primary objective. In this way we get a brief taste of a neighboring country so that we might pay it a proper visit at some future time. We don't become confused, because we only make a brief visit, rarely staying a night. This is also a good technique if you are of a mind to "collect countries." I well remember the evening we made an hour drive from the Bodensee in Bavaria to have dinner in Liechtenstein. How many people do you know who have visited that tiny country – or who even know where it is? I can hear the sound of your feet as you run for a gazetteer. Certainly, when I visit Luxembourg with Nancy or other traveling companions, I only stay for a few days. Even though they are tolerant of my roots research, I don't want to impose on them. On occasion I have begun or ended a trip with a week alone just to do family research.

If your finances are rather limited, you will want to select a country where the cost of food and lodging are low. Spain and Portugal fit that bill very nicely. They are not third world countries, but are still recovering from the developmental depression that they brought on themselves four centuries ago when they lived on the wealth of the New World. Prices are reasonable in the larger cities, and are quite low in small towns – if you look for bargains. For example, we once stopped for the night at a small village south of Santiago de Compostela in Spain. The hotel was new and spacious. It had a public sitting room and a large balcony for sitting in the sun. The cost of the room was the equivalent of $25 a night. At that price we didn't complain that breakfast was not included.

When to plan

When do you start planning a trip? It seems to me – personal taste – that you can never begin too early. I usually start planning a new trip when I have returned from one and have rested up for a few days. It takes time to research literature and to let the ideas settle into my memory bank. Besides, the best time to make reservations for flights, transportation and lodging is just after the first of the year. At this time the schedules and prices are set, and there are abundant openings. On the other hand, it is amazing how full facilities can be if you delay your commitment until March or later.

What to see and do
Now that you have selected the country you want to visit, you must decide what is of primary interest to you in that country. Your passion might be genealogy, or history, or scenery, or sports, or the arts, or nightlife, or loafing, or people. Your itinerary should reflect this passion. Another caution is important here. If your travel partners have varying interests, you need to include something for everyone.

Brainstorm with your travel partners. Share ideas. Plan alternate itineraries in the larger cities. Just because some of you love museums and others love to shop doesn't mean you have to choose one activity in place of the other. Besides, the person who doesn't participate in the planning is someone who very well might complain when you are traveling. Have a care. Certainly, if you expect to do serious genealogical research in a library or an archive, you want to have some optional activities planned for your traveling companions.

It is easy for your little group to split up to do different things. It is especially easy in large cities, which tend to have excellent public transportation. One other advantage of splitting up occasionally is that you can then compare notes to see if you want to repeat the adventure of the people who went somewhere different from you.

When to go
There are twelve months of the year in which you can travel. When you do so depends on what you want to do. If your passion is skiing, you won't go in July. If your passion is sea and surf, you won't go in December. Okay, so those ideas are obvious. Now, when should you go? It depends upon what you want to do, what kind of weather you hope to have, when transportation costs are reasonable, and when the world is full of other tourists, such as from June through August.

The weather in continental Europe is reasonably comfortable in May and October, and quite comfortable for all of the months in between. It can be hot on occasion in the summer. If you don't plan to stay in major hotel chains (expensive!) and are sensitive to heat, avoid July and August, since modestly priced hotels don't have air conditioning.

In general, it is best to go when tourism is just out of season. Few things will be closed. The weather won't be much different from high season. The prices of lodging and food might be a bit lower. But, best of all, the crowds will be down. You can actually see things. Off season we were able to tour the royal chateau at Fontainebleau in comfort. At another time, during high season, we were elbow to elbow with crushing crowds. Have you ever been jabbed in the ribs by a Japanese camera?

The cost of air fare is quite seasonal. If cost is a consideration for you, as it is for us, then you want to avoid leaving between June 1 and September 1. Most tourists want to travel during those times. The airlines charge a premium because they have no difficulty selling tickets. Before June and after August, fares become lower. In cold months the fares become bargain basement.

So, if you want to visit London and do the theaters and museums, your best bet is to travel during the winter. The weather will be cold, but not extreme, because of the Gulf Current. No problem. You will be spending most of your time indoors.

If you plan to do sea and surf, and are concerned about crowds and flight costs, then you want to travel to the Mediterranean in May or September. The best and most reliable weather will be found on the coasts of Spain and Italy.

If you plan to do scenery in the northern part of Europe, you will want to avoid May. It tends to be rainy then. In Ireland, Scotland, Belgium and Luxembourg it can rain at any time of the year. This is another legacy of the Gulf Current. Scotland can have miserably wet and cool weather even in the summer, but it rarely freezes in the winter. Believe it or not, there is a castle in Scotland that has palm trees in its garden.

Of course, the Europeans know all of this. They plan their travel accordingly. In late May and June the roads of Europe are full of Hollanders heading south with small trailers, which they call caravans. They are seeking sun and warmth. Germans tend to travel in June and July. The French go on vacation in August – most of the French, for all of August. What does that do to the availability of lodging? Not much. The hotels are always full of Americans all summer anyway.

We usually travel from the middle of April through the middle of May. There are a number of reasons for this. Air transportation is below the premium rate, especially for senior citizens. The weather is reasonably pleasant and springlike, with only occasional showers. The tourist crush has not yet begun. The tourist sites are open and operating. Hotel rooms are easy to find without the need to make advance reservations. All in all, it is a great time to travel in comfort and with maximum flexibility. Our second choice is to travel in October. The weather is a bit less reliable, but the color of the trees adds to the beauty.

One more thought about timing as it relates to genealogical research. If you travel off season, then the staff in city halls and national archives will have fewer customers demanding their attention. The less the hustle and bustle, the more they are likely to spend time helping you with your research.

How long to stay

Now that you have decided where to go and when to do so, you must decide how long you want to stay. That is another very personal decision. If you go for less than a week, you will have little opportunity to obtain value from the cost of air fare. From personal experience, I would recommend at least two weeks. If you have elderly parents or family members with ill health, you might want to limit your trip to two weeks. Worry and guilt tend to build up. If you plan to be gone for more than two weeks, you would be well advised to rent an apartment or a house and settle in for a while. Moving around tends to develop a creeping fatigue that becomes quite noticeable after three weeks.

Our preference is to plan trips of two to three weeks. I prefer three weeks. Nancy prefers two weeks. So, I begin planning a trip of two weeks duration. Then, when she agrees to the agenda, I tell her of wonderful little add-ons we could have if we just spent another day or two. The trip usually winds up to be about 18 to 20 days. Then Nancy's bookkeeper background begins to come into play. She wants to travel on weekends. Flights tend to be over-booked on those days. This opens the opportunity for accepting a bump, taking a later flight, and receiving a voucher for about the amount of money it will cost to fly next year. More about this in Chapter 4.

To give you an idea what one of our trips is like, I'll take a moment here to describe the trip that we planned for 1998. We left on May 17 and returned on June 7 – both Sundays – flying to Paris. We began the trip with two days in a wonderful inn in Bacharach, Germany on the Rhine. We toured the castles that adorn every hilltop along both sides of the river. If you look at a map, you will see that this area of the Rhine borders on France, and is just south of Luxembourg. On the way to the Rhine, we spent one night in Luxembourg, my ancestral home. We had dinner and a chat with cousins of mine.

From the Rhine we drove to southwest France, to the Dordogne River valley. It is a beautiful bit of country, and is where prehistoric man painted animals on the walls and ceilings of caves. Ever hear of Lascaux? The paintings are really art, and must be seen in place to be fully appreciated. In Dordogne we stayed in a 400-year-old farmhouse that we rented for six people – ourselves, Jack and June, and Jacques and Michèle. And yes, it was the American who rented the house, not the Frenchman. The rental was quite modest at $450 total for the six of us. But notice another reason why we travel just ahead of the prime tourist season. The rent of that house doubles after the first of June.

After Dordogne, we spent four days on a pilot-it-yourself barge on the Burgundy Canal which passes through Dijon, France. We ended with an afternoon and a night in Fontainebleau. Of course, there were a few stop offs for a night of two in interesting places between these major events. Sound nice to you? You can do the same with a little planning effort. Read on.

Oh yes, don't plan to spend too much contiguous time in genealogical research. I have always found it nice to spend a few days on research, and then to take some time for other activities while I assimilate what I have gathered. This makes the next session of research more productive. It would be a shame to return from a long trip only to learn that you failed to make use of some new information. Normally you can't fly right back to fill in the voids.

Sources of information

There are wonderful sources of information with which to plan a trip. The first thing to do is to go to a good book store and buy a map of the country that you plan to visit. A large scale map with a scale of 1:200,000 is ideal for planning. You might consider buying a book of maps of all of Europe. This is a real economy if you expect to visit a number of countries in future years. European maps identify points of historic or scenic interest. The name of the location of interest might be printed in a yellow box to highlight it, or there might be a star printed next to the name. The south of France and Germany, and the coasts of northern countries, are full of stars.

Visit a travel bureau. They have racks full of literature about tours to various countries. Pick up a handful that interest you. Don't feel guilty. Who knows, one of the tours might attract you. Each tour lists the places that are on its itinerary. Jot down the names and locations of those places that seem of most interest to you. This is a great starting point for planning your own private agenda. While you are at the tourist office, explain to them what you are planning, and ask for a train schedule for the country you will be visiting.

Now you are ready to go to a library, or better yet, to that book store where you bought the map. If it is a first class book store, you can buy a cup of coffee, pick up a few guidebooks from the rack, and sit down for some serious browsing. Make notes of added places of interest. Also note the guidebooks that seem most to your taste. I personally prefer the ones with lots of pictures of things to see. At some point in your planning you will buy a few of them. A great place to buy guidebooks at bargain prices is in an outlet that specializes in publisher overruns. Yes, the prices of hotels and restaurants are out of date, but the descriptions of tourist attractions rarely change from printing to printing. Mountains, castles and cities don't move around much.

While you have your nose in maps and guidebooks, jot down the addresses of tourist offices of the country you plan to visit. If you write to them, you will receive piles of wonderful planning material. Don't panic if you don't receive it promptly. The material is usually not printed until about the end of each year. If you have access to an embassy or a consulate, you should be able to pick up some literature at any time you wish, even before the end of the year.

After you have done a reasonable amount of reading, you might want to ask around for the names of people who travel a lot. These people normally love to talk about their trips. As they talk, they actually relive the trip and enjoy it all over again. The more you already know about the places they discuss, the more they will tell you, and the more you will appreciate the information and remember it.

To prove that this is a modern book, I must advise you to search the Internet for travel information. Since the Internet is a simple and inexpensive medium for advertising, many countries, tourist offices, hotels, restaurants and other facilities have developed home pages. The problem is how to find what you are looking for in such a forest of seemingly random information. The search engines, such as Locos and Yahoo are improving, however. One of the newest, fastest, and best is called Google. To give you an example of the power of Internet, we have used it to find and rent vacation houses, to rent a barge, to buy train tickets, to reserve hotels, and to print maps so that we could find interesting places that are off the beaten track.

Certainly, if you are a serious genealogist, you will want to visit centers of research in your own country to learn about the things you might look for when on European soil. Study some standard texts on how to do research. Read your own records. Make a list of the villages where your family lived. Plot these locations on a map to help plan driving routes. Make a list of the churches that your family attended. There might be some records there that aren't available here. Make a list of the names or addresses of houses in which your family lived. You will certainly want to take photographs, and possibly interview the current residents. The names of houses tend to remain those of the people who built them, no matter how much time has passed.

If you merely want to make contact with the land of your ancestry, you still will need to do some preliminary study. See if somewhere – possibly in the family Bible or on an old family document – there is a record of the village, the city, or even the general area where your ancestors lived. That is a place you will enjoy visiting.

Managing time

As you plan your agenda, you want to fill it up with more things than you can possibly do – about 50% more. The expanded agenda gives you options in case you are unable to do something that you had your heart set on. This can happen due to travel delays, occasional bad weather, unexpected closing hours, etc. Don't expect to do everything that you have on your agenda. Do expect to experience some things that you didn't have on the agenda. The people you meet and the signs you encounter are wonderful travel guides.

Travel time can vary greatly. Flights can be delayed. Jet lag can strike for a while and reduce the amount of touring you are capable of doing for a day or two. Trains are good about running on time in Europe, but they don't necessarily run at the time you want. Average speed on European roads varies widely. As you plan to drive from one place to another, allow for an average of 110 km per hour (70 mph) average speed on expressways, and 60 km per hour (40 mph) on side roads. Average speed can be even less on mountain roads and in Portugal, where the side roads don't seem to have had much maintenance since the Romans left. If you are driving through or around a major city, even on an expressway, you might add a few hours to your plan because of rush hour traffic. One very nice thing is that there is little maintenance delay on expressways in Europe. The construction standards are more stringent than in the U.S., and the weather extremes are less severe. The highways don't need as much maintenance.

Be prepared, however, for traffic jams on expressways. They sometimes happen due to holiday crushes, accidents, and other acts of God. We have experienced delays of several hours. This is a good opportunity for a picnic if you are prepared.

Read, read, read

Now read, read, and if you can, read some more. The more information you can absorb, the better your trip will be. First of all, you will select the best sites to visit. Second, you will know more about them, and will gain more from the experience. Third, you will reduce the possibility of unpleasant surprises. Besides, it is very difficult to appreciate a marvelous old building if you have your nose in a guidebook.

Lay out an outline of your trip on paper. Annotate it and change it as you plan. Plan your trip day by day, noting the day of the week as well as the date. The things you want to emphasize in your reading are the cities and towns; the points of interest, and their operating hours. The things you don't need to read are the descriptions of hotels and restaurants. They are everywhere. The ones in a guidebook are the ones that the publisher likes, or the ones that paid a fee to be included. (The Michelin guides are a notable exception, famous for their reliability.) Chapters 8 and 9 discuss lodging and food in some depth. While you are reading guidebooks, read these chapters too.

Visas

While you are doing all of this reading, look carefully in the guidebooks to see if a visa is required in any of the countries that you plan to visit. It would be a disaster to arrive at the airport or the border of a country only to find out that you are not allowed in for lack of a visa. I know of no country in western Europe that requires a visa. However, one is generally required in any Eastern Block country. You will have to submit your passport and a properly filled out form to obtain a visa. The time to process your application will generally be from one to six weeks. Another good reason to plan ahead.

Turkey requires a visa for visitors from the U.S., but not from most countries in western Europe. I believe it is that country's way of getting even with us for requiring a visa for visitors to the U.S. from most other countries, including Turkey. Fair is fair.

How to spend a rainy day

Nancy and I were on our first visit to Jack and June's summer home on a lake in Michigan. Since Phoenix is extremely hot in the summer, they found a bargain house (lucky dogs!) on a lake near Traverse City. They had great expectations that we would spend the three day visit playing in the lake. It rained. It rained. For three days it rained. With no other water distractions available, we began to talk about Europe. I was carrying some literature, since I was already planning next summer's trip.

Within three days we had that next trip fairly well laid out, and we had recruited two superb traveling companions. We all have thanked the good Lord for sending that rain. Most trips aren't planned that quickly. The advantage of this trip was that for the most part we were visiting places where Nancy and I had already been.

Operating hours

Operating hours are a particular point of concern if you have your heart set on experiencing something special and have limited time. A

few examples will illustrate this. All of the following information is available in traditional guidebooks..
- The Passion Play at Oberammergau only takes place every ten years.
- The Louvre in Paris is closed on Tuesdays.
- The cave at Lascaux is closed on Mondays.
- The open air market at Ventimiglia (the Tijuana of Italy) operates only on Friday.
- Various local markets operate only on Saturday or Sunday

Now you know why you noted the day of the week on each day of your agenda.

Be flexible

Failure to read about a locale can cause interesting surprises, sometimes good and sometimes bad. On a trip to Spain we decided to visit Gibraltar. As long as we were visiting the rock, we decided that we might as well take a ferry across the Mediterranean to see a bit of Morocco. We hadn't prepared for this other than to read a single guidebook. The editor of this particular book seems to think that all cities are beautiful and charming. Not true. It turned out that Gibraltar has little charm, and that the nearest port in Africa is Sueta, an unimpressive Spanish city on a piece of land that Spain had conquered several centuries ago. All was saved when a local travel guide offered us a reasonably priced bus trip and – horrors – a guided tour of the Moroccan city of Tetuan. It worked out quite well.

Special days

While you are at the library or the consulate, ask for information on national holidays, celebrations and feast days. Depending on what you want to experience, you need to plan around them. Any good guidebook will tell you about national holidays. In Latin countries there are often parades and processions on significant religious holidays. They are charming and colorful if that is what you are there for. If not, then they can tie up traffic pretty thoroughly and prevent you from being somewhere else. If you like large celebrations and don't mind crowds, you might want to be in Paris on July 14 for Bastille Day. I don't. If you do, then make sure to have your lodging booked well in advance. I'd hate to have you included among the homeless. If you want to experience the Passion Play at Oberammergau, Germany, you will need to make reservations for two nights at a local bed-and-breakfast.

If you want to avoid crowds, road jams, and scarcity of facilities, plan to avoid travel during national holidays and celebrations. If you can't avoid them, you can at least plan to be off the beaten track during that time. For example, the feast of the Ascension is a holiday in Catholic countries. Tourist sites will be fuller at that time, especially if the feast falls near a weekend. If you stay in small towns and villages, no problem. If you plan to stay at a prime tourist site, you might experience a housing shortage.

Now, I will be the first to admit that I am occasionally caught by a holiday. On these occasions, it helps to have a sense of humor and to be able to go with the flow. Most small hotels will help you find lodging somewhere else if they are full.

Chapter 3
Packing

How much to pack?

How much should I pack for a trip to Europe? What should I be prepared for? What can I do if I find that I am missing something I need? And the answers are:

    Much, much less than you might think.
    Most anything.
    Buy it, or do without.

This is all part of the great adventure. Just think how you can brag about your self-sufficiency when you get home. Seriously, you can travel light and do quite well in Europe – if you do it wisely. Read on to gain wisdom.

Packing for a trip is always a compromise between bulk/weight and style/convenience. This chapter will tell you how much of the latter you can obtain within the constraints of the former. The problem is in making the tough decisions that are required. I know travelers who make no decisions at all. They just pack everything that they might conceivably need. I have friends who pack about four times more for an overnight trip than we do for three weeks in Europe. You must remember that the trunks on European cars are small. They aren't built to handle unlimited luggage.

There is an old story about how to pack for a trip abroad. It says that you should lay out on a bed all of the clothes and money that you think you might need. Then pack the clothes, pick up the suitcases, and carry them around the block. When you return, exhausted, put away half of the clothes and double the amount of money. Pack again, and walk again. Repeat this procedure until you can make it around the block without being fatigued. There is more truth than fancy in this little story.

John's and Margie's drawers

"John's and Margie's Drawers." Now isn't that a heading that piques your interest? The point to be made here is simple. Like many retired people, particularly those who have children that live in other places, John and Margie travel a lot. They have an interesting technique for ensuring that they don't forget anything important when they pack for a trip. They each have a drawer that is dedicated to their travel clothes and appropriate incidentals. When they return home from a trip the clothing is laundered and returned to the drawers. They are always ready to travel.

What do I need?

The things you need for a trip are really minimal. You need enough clothes to last the trip, to adapt to changes in the weather, and to handle a modest variety of social contacts. You need things that you cannot do without – money, plane tickets, passports, and prescription medications. Anything else can be done without or purchased on-site. If, however, you are traveling for a sporting activity such as diving, skiing, biking or mountain climbing, you certainly will need a significant amount of gear for that activity. You will find no help here for such a trip. We have no experience in that area. The ideas in this chapter relate only to touring activities.

Each person needs five containers (notice that I didn't say pieces of luggage) for carrying essentials. The first container is a small suitcase for the bulk of your clothes and materials. If you hate waiting for luggage to be unloaded from the airplane, you might find it convenient to obtain the type of suitcase that stewardesses use – small, and with wheels and a handle. The second container is a generous purse or briefcase. In this you carry all non-vital documents, minimal grooming materials, one change of underclothing, breakable items, and a few miscellaneous things that might set off the alarm when you pass through the x-ray machine at the airport. The third container is a modest-sized nylon bag that you pack into the bottom of the suitcase. You will use it to carry the dirty clothes that you will accumulate, and to make room in the suitcase for the trinkets that you will certainly buy during the trip. The fourth container is a security wallet for carrying passports, credit cards and money. The fifth container is your own body. You can save a lot of packing space by wearing the bulkiest pieces of clothing, such as a jacket or sports coat, walking shoes, and possibly a sweater. This also insulates you against the chill that seems to be the normal operating temperature of an airplane cabin when in flight.

Notice, that even with five "containers" you can avoid checking your luggage into the cargo hold if that is your wish. The next chapter contains a few thoughts about the pros and cons of carry-on versus check-in luggage.

Lost luggage

One time early in my travels I was sent by my employer to visit several European facilities. The trip began in Brussels and continued on to Leicester and Glasgow. It was a wonderful experience, both professionally and culturally. But on the flight between Brussels and Leicester my check-in luggage (all of my clothes) disappeared. The plane had made a single stop in Birmingham, England. I was convinced that the luggage was there.

At each facility that I visited the secretaries tried to locate the luggage, but to no avail. Of course, I was forced to purchase some clothing. I tried to minimize expense and limited the outer wear to two dress shirts and two pairs of trousers. With grooming items and some underclothes, this all fit in a small shoulder bag about the size of a lady's purse. I was never inconvenienced. The airline eventually reimbursed me. I still have two favorite shirts that are of British make.

My luggage eventually showed up (from Birmingham) on the day I was to leave Glasgow. I carried home a suitcase that I had never opened. The point in all of this is that you can travel with an absolute minimum of luggage if you really need to, or want to.

Clothing

Experience has taught us that we always, no matter how carefully we plan, bring home items of clothing that have not been used on the trip. These "just in case" items must be kept to a minimum. There are three reasons for extra items – style, grime, and comfort. Normally you don't have to worry too much about style. Most people that you meet won't know you and won't ever see you again. You are unlikely to be asked to attend a high-style event where you would be embarrassed by being underdressed. The less clothing you carry, the simpler your choices of what to put on in the morning.

I attended a wedding in Europe, and I packed a lightweight suit. If you plan to attend the opera, you might want one really nice outfit. Fortunately most dressy outfits for women are lightweight. For men it only takes a dress shirt and a tie under the sports coat that was worn on the plane.

There are two easy ways to handle soiled clothes. The first is to wear jeans. Nobody ever notices that they are dirty unless they are *really* dirty. Jeans are always in style in Europe now, even in nice restaurants, and even, occasionally, at the opera. The other way to handle soiled clothes is the one we prefer, especially since we don't really care for jeans. Generation gap? We pack things that can be rinsed out and can be expected to dry overnight. It is amazing how a few minutes at a sink each evening can keep you fresh, and can keep your suitcase free of the clutter of dirty clothes. We really don't want to use that nylon bag until we are on the way home.

Presuming that you will select clothes that are comfortable, let's talk here only about comfort as it relates to the weather. A thin, waterproof jacket or a folding umbrella will go a long way toward protecting you from rain. And you will experience rain unless you are visiting a desert country. The most practical way to protect yourself from changes in temperature is to carry layers. Don't pack heavy clothing in case of cold weather. Pack layers. You will want to have a lightweight sweater to wear under your jacket. You will want a warm undershirt. In this way, you are ready for sun or snow. All you have to do is to add or subtract a layer.

Dark colored clothing is more practical than light colored, since it doesn't show spots or smudges as readily. And men, brace yourself for this last idea. You would do well to pack silk or nylon underclothing. It rinses out easily and dries overnight.

You might consider a few additional items of clothing if they are important to you, and if you find the room in your luggage. Just remember, since dirty clothing always takes up more luggage space than clean clothing does, you would do well to leave a little space unfilled. You might want a sweat suit for lounging in the evening. You might want a pair of slippers for the same reason. They feel nice on the feet during a flight if you have packed them in your briefcase or purse. You might give consideration to an inflatable neck pillow made for airplane passengers. It is amazingly comfortable. If you have a light nylon or silk robe, you might find it handy when you are at a hotel where the toilet and bathing facilities are located down the hall.

A second pair of shoes can come in handy, especially for women. They take up a lot of room, however. I personally prefer to take only the pair that I am wearing. If I run into a problem, I can always buy another pair on-site. This need has never developed. Think of the inconvenience I have avoided! Gym shoes are seldom worn by Europeans, and will label you as an American tourist. However, the younger generation is now tending toward gym shoes as a style item. Good walking shoes are the best. They wear well. They protect you from injury on rough, cobblestone streets in medieval villages. Finally, they make you look more like a European, at least a European tourist.

The art of packing

We were at Jack's and June's house in Phoenix and were completing plans for our first trip together. June could not imagine how she could travel with only one suitcase. She knew that there was no way she could survive. Nancy tried to explain how it was done, but to no avail. Finally the two of them retired to the bedroom and began rummaging through drawers and closets.

After a while they emerged with a single suitcase. June's eyes shone as she cried, "We did it!" She traveled with that suitcase, and unpacked and repacked several more times without need of help. When we came home, she found that she had not used all of her clothes, and had added a number of purchases to the load. No problem.

Grooming

Grooming materials can take up a lot of space. Luggage manufacturers even offer small suitcases specially designed to hold them. These suitcases are best left on the shelf in the store, since they add needless bulk. This is a good time to remind you again that you are unlikely to meet anyone you know. You don't have to look like a work of art. If indeed you plan to meet people that you know, and if they are friends, they will be well aware that you are traveling and that you should not be expected to be the epitome of sartorial splendor. If you follow this rule, you will eliminate a lot of needless junk. I travel with a toothbrush, a small tube of toothpaste, a small underarm deodorant, a comb, a small bottle of shampoo, and a couple of disposable razors. Nancy wears her hair short, and isn't inclined to a lot of makeup. Her requirements are similar. All of this fits easily into a "shaving kit" in our suitcase.

The grooming items that really consume space in your luggage are those which are electrically operated, such as razors and hair dryers. If you can possibly do without them, you will save a lot of space and bother. If you cannot do without them, remember that you will also need to buy and pack a power convertor. European electricity generally comes at 220 volts and 50 cycles, as compared to our 110 volts and 60 cycles. The voltage will incinerate your appliance unless it is converted. The cycles will just make it run at a slower speed. Jacques, from France, worked for a few years in the U.S. He bought a garage door opener here. It works fine, but he has the slowest garage door in town. Some items, such as a Norelco razor are made in Europe and will operate on European current. Be sure to read the instructions that come with the device. You can buy an adaptor plug rather cheaply at any good luggage store. Remember that different countries have different plug conventions. By the way, if you plan to stay at three to five-star hotels, then you can expect to find a hair dryer provided with the room.

There are several other grooming items that you should pack: a washcloth and a bar of soap in a waterproof container. Some hotels below three-star quality do not provide wash cloths. German hotels below three star do not provide soap. I have never been able to learn why.

Oh yes, if you only carry the shoes that you are wearing, you will want to pack a small container of powder to combat odor and perspiration buildup. It is a minor courtesy to your travel companions.

Medications

You should always pack an adequate supply of prescription medications. Don't forget a copy of the prescription and your doctor's telephone number. To avoid any serious concern about language difficulties, you might also want to pack a minimal amount of non-prescription medications. The critical items are aspirin, sleeping pills, and something for diarrhea. Hopefully you will never need these medications. But if you do, you don't want to have to take the time to hunt for a pharmacy. You can generally avoid diarrhea by exercising some care in what you eat and drink. This is described in Chapter 8. Even so, some people have stomachs that are extemely sensitive to any change in diet, no matter how sanitary and tasty.

There are a few additional items that you might find convenient to have on hand. These include a small, a very small, first aid kit, and a supply of small paper towels, soaked in alcohol. This is the type of thing that is supplied in casinos to help slot machine players clean their hands after losing all of their money. You might also want to include a small container of tissues for runny noses, and a small packet of toilet tissue. These are items that you would tend to carry on a trip in the U.S. Other things to consider are matches or a lighter, rubber bands, suntan oil, and a sewing kit and crazy glue for instant repairs. A small flashlight can be handy at night. All of these small things can be packed in a single container so that you can find them when you need them.

Be sure to carry a card with your frequent flier identification number. It is amazing how many times a ticket clerk or a car rental clerk forgets to ask for your number, or how many times you forget to give it. You will want to be sure to get credit for your air miles so that you can take a "free" trip to Europe later. Another thing we have found quite handy to carry is a set of adhesive labels already addressed to those people to whom we plan to send post cards. It certainly speeds up the writing of cards.

Documents

Of course you will carry personal identification, drivers licenses, passports, airplane tickets, ATM card and charge cards. Nobody needs to be reminded of this – or do they? The check-in desk at the airline will make sure that you have photo identification, passport and ticket before they allow you to board the plane. Everything else is up to you. Do you know whether your ATM and charge cards will work outside the U.S.? We had a nasty surprise on our first trip after my retirement. You would be wise to check out your cards.

Consider investing in an international drivers license. It will cost you about $12, and is good insurance against possible frustration and delay on the road. In most countries the police can't read any language except their own. The international drivers license tells them in their own language that you are authorized to drive in their country. You can obtain such a license from automobile insurance associations, such as the American Automobile Association and the Chicago Motor Club. You don't have to be a member of the organization to buy an international drivers license from it. The license is valid for a year from whatever effective date you specify.

You will want to carry a copy of any contract that you have negotiated for such things as hotel or train reservations or for auto rental. In fact, you want to make an photocopy of them. Put one copy in your suitcase. Put the other in your purse or briefcase. This will save a lot of problems if the originals are lost. It will avoid other problems too. Sometimes the European agency will want to keep the original document. They are the originators of bureaucracy and red tape. These banes of civilization were not invented by the American Indian. I have found that European branches of auto agencies might want to charge me more than the contract called for. With a copy of the original contract, I can sometimes avoid the extra charges. If not, I have always received a prompt and courteous explanation and/or refund when I returned home. Of course, I had to provide a copy of the documents signed at the rental desk in Europe.

As long as you are copying documents, copy a few more. God willing, you will never need them. They are a minimal expense, and don't take up much space in your luggage. Copy the identification pages in your passport. It will help expedite obtaining a new one from a local U.S. embassy if your original is lost. Copy your drivers licenses, domestic and international. You will not be able to obtain a replacement in Europe, but you can at least prove the existence of the original. Make a copy of the receipt for your travelers checks, the document that lists the serial numbers of the checks. Finally, copy your airline tickets and train tickets. These copies should be carried in different pieces of luggage from the ones in which the originals are kept. You might want to exchange the copies with your traveling partners as an added precaution against loss.

It sometimes helps not to speak the language

We were planning a trip to Spain. One travel guidebook explained that the Spanish police were very concerned about drivers being insured. The book said that the prudent driver obtained a "yellow card" that verified insurance coverage. Without it, he faced a heavy fine. Twice I asked the car rental agency about this, explaining that we had insurance coverage through our credit card agency. Twice I was assured that the car rental desk in Madrid would automatically provide me with the necessary card.

Of course, when the time came to pick up the car, I forgot to ask about the card. Of course, the rental clerk did too. Several weeks later, near the end of our trip, we remembered the card and speculated about what our exposure might be.

Sure enough, the next day we were waved to the side of the highway by a police officer. He spoke only Spanish. Concerned about our situation, I forgot almost all of my limited Spanish vocabulary – a fortunate occurrence. The officer wanted our car title. Easy to understand. We showed him the rental contract. "Your verification of insurance?" He gave an expressive and disdainful shrug when I showed him my credit card. "Your driving license?" Jack, who was driving, showed his international drivers license. This seemed to surprise and please the officer. He thought a moment and then waved us on our way. I think he was happy to be rid of us. The feeling was mutual.

Security wallet

Your most important documents, the originals that is, should be carried in some sort of security wallet. These simple wallets come in four varieties. The most common, and most obvious, is the "fanny pack" which is tied around your waist and is worn outside your clothing. I don't like the fanny pack for three reasons. It is bulky and uncomfortable when you sit. It brands you as an obvious tourist. And it advertizes to the world where your valuables are.

The other three varieties of security wallet are all worn under your clothing. They are flat and invisible unless you stuff them with too many things. One type ties around your waist. Another hangs on a loop around your neck. A third resembles a shoulder holster, being supported by a strap over the shoulder and lying at your side under your arm. I personally prefer this last type, because I am generally unaware that it is there. It is, however, the most difficult to access when you need something from it. But after all, who ever heard of good security that did not carry with it some degree of inconvenience? Speaking of security, any purse should have a shoulder strap. It helps avoid theft, and it leaves the arms free.

At about this point you are asking yourself if it is safe to travel in Europe. The answer is "yes," but with some qualifications. There are places in Europe that are unsafe, just as there are in our own country. Generally you are safer in Europe than you are at home. Most of western Europe is free from large ghettos of poverty. Where they exist, they tend to be off the tourist route. Police surveillance is more obvious in Europe than in the U.S. In places where there is a risk, it is one of theft, not violence. I was once robbed of my travelers checks by some waifs in Rome. The only real loss was to my pride. The poorer the country, and the closer it is to the Mediterranean, the more the risk of theft. Use your security wallet, travel in pairs, and avoid wearing expensive jewelry. Don't even pack any inexpensive jewelry if it looks expensive. You will really be safer than you are in a strange city in the U.S. More on this in Chapter 17.

What do you put in the security wallet? You put in it your passport, credit cards, travelers checks, drivers licenses, and any cash in excess of the equivalent of $100. To avoid excessive "undressing" in public, I carry in my wallet about $100 in the local currency and one travelers check.

Money

As long as we are talking about money, how much and what kind should you pack? How high did that pile on the bed get to be? The amount of money you carry depends on how expensively you plan to travel. We travel modestly, sleeping in two-star hotels, and eating only our evening meal in restaurants. For this reason, we travel for about $75 per person per day, total cost, including air fare. You have your own style.

If you are comfortable using charge cards, you can pay for most, but not all, hotels and restaurant meals by charge card. You can use a charge card or an ATM card to obtain cash when needed. Thus you can usually get along with a few thousand dollars in "cash." I always carry $2000 in travelers checks of $100 denomination. There is a lot more on this subject in Chapter 15. The important thing here is to avoid having so many travelers checks in your security wallet that you walk around looking lumpy.

If you plan to travel in Germany, you might want to carry more travelers checks. The Germans have not yet become addicted to "plastic money." They generally expect payment in cash.

Genealogy aids

If you want to experience some of what your ancestors did, you should take a list of villages and cities where you know your ancestors lived. If you don't have that information, at least mark a map with the area that you think they came from. Take along any old photos or documents that you might want to show to somebody in Europe in order to try to learn a bit more about your family. If you are a dedicated genealogist, you want to take a copy of your family tree (the Old Country portion) and the names and addresses of any known heraldry and genealogy experts. If you know the names of any houses where your ancestors lived, be sure to take them along so that you can see and photograph the houses.

Miscellaneous items

There are a few miscellaneous items that the prudent traveler considers carrying. They are described here in no particular order of importance.

Camera and film. I hate cameras, because on my first few trips I took so many photos that I had to wait for them to be developed before I could see where I had been. My wife, however, wants to keep a photo or two, and she wants me to take them. I used to carry a small, foolproof but not "Geneproof," self-adjusting 35 mm camera. Recently I have changed to a digital camera. It is great for viewing a photo as soon as it is taken. That way I can be assured that I have a satisfactory image of a person or place that I might never see again. You might want something fancier, or even a video camera. It is a matter of personal taste and passion. Remember though, you have to carry whatever you choose. I have seen people pull out a video camera on a plane to make a record of all the people they traveled with. These camera pests make enemies at a great rate. Plan to carry all of the film that you expect to use. You can buy film readily in Europe, but it often comes with development cost included. This is a convenience that you are unlikely to take advantage of, because you will probably be moving around. If you have a digital camera, be sure to take along several sets of batteries, a charger, and a power convertor for European current.

Carry an extra set of keys for the car that you left at home, unless you had a ride to the airport. Carry the keys in the briefcase or purse so that your pockets are free to hold a generous supply of foreign coins.

Pack away some U.S. coins in case you find need to use the telephone when you reach the airport on your return. If your airport of departure has a currency exchange desk, you might want to obtain a bit ($100) of the currency of your target country. It is always nice to have some cash on hand, even though you can get it on arrival, and even though you "pay through the nose" for currency exchange at any airport. I keep about ten $1 bills in my wallet for tips in case I am ever short of small coins and bills in the local currency. Nobody ever refuses U.S. banknotes as a tip.

If you are a heavy sleeper and plan to keep any sort of schedule, carry a small, battery-powered alarm clock. I get along easily with a wrist watch alarm. Never carry a clock that needs alternating current.

It will require a power converter, and a mathematics professor to calculate the time conversion because of 50 vs 60 cycles.

We usually carry a few tapes of musical favorites, because we get tired of local radio programs while driving. Sometimes we have carried a small tape recorder in case the car doesn't have a tape player. Lately we have tended to get away from this, because we found the need for the recorder to be minimal. What is your taste?

Here is a miscellaneous list of items to consider packing. A puzzle book, a magazine, or a good novel (paperback) are handy for use on the plane or for bedside reading. A small pocket knife has many uses, especially for cutting cheese on the picnics that we will talk about later. A corkscrew and bottle opener are also very useful on picnics. My wife even packs a pair of small, unbreakable cups for those picnics. Plastic glasses tend to blow over with any kind of breeze. She also packs a small nylon cooler bag to hold fruit and cheese for our picnics.

A notebook and ballpoint pen are handy for taking an occasional note so that you can remember where you were and what you took photos of. You will also want to keep a list of the gifts and souvenirs that you buy, and their prices. Uncle Sam will ask you for that information on your return.

A coin purse is very handy for carrying the many coins that you will want to accumulate. Europeans are more inclined to use coins – in denominations up to the equivalent of $3. Plastic bags are convenient for storing dirty clothes, leftover food (not in the same bag,) and other small items that might otherwise lose themselves in the car or in the luggage.

Carry a list of phone numbers that might come in handy. This includes the office of your airline in any country in which you plan to travel. Carry the phone number of your physician, and of members of your family. The physician is important in case you have any kind of medical emergency. The family is important so that you can occasionally verify that they are all right. The family are also important in case you run out of money.

Finally, you will want to carry a few maps, a guidebook or two, and a compass. European roads and streets are not designed to line up with the four main points of the compass. They tend to follow old cow paths, the route of least resistance. If you find a straight road, it is probably laid upon a foundation that was first established by the Roman army.

On one trip two different people broke or lost their prescription glasses. It would be prudent to pack, carefully, a spare set. Don't forget your sunglasses. If they are prescription, you might be able to do without the spare set.

Where is north?

Jerry and Mary were driving through the countryside south of Paris. The roads and the maps didn't always seem to be quite in synch. They couldn't find the specific road that they were looking for. After a while Mary commented that the water tower they were passing looked familiar. In the next half hour, they found themselves passing "other" water towers that were quite similar, in fact, identical.

This realization assisted Mary in convincing Jerry to do what all wives request and all husbands resist. He stopped and asked for directions. Jerry was so horrified at this breach of traditional male independence, that he now makes sure he has a compass available on the dashboard. I personally don't need one. Nancy has an uncanny sense of direction. Ticks me off. It is a "man thing."

Gifts

If you plan to visit any friends or acquaintances in Europe, carry a few gifts. American or Canadian bourbon is always appreciated, because it is very expensive in Europe. Wine is never appreciated, because Europeans are convinced, often with good reason, that they know more about wine and have better wine than we do. Candy is a nice present, but it tends to melt. A coffee table book about the U.S. is a great gift for someone who has never lived here for any length of time. Unfortunately, all of these things are rather heavy.

If you can find something that is truly American, it will be more appreciated than an item that can easily be purchased in any country. An example would be a piece of scrimshaw. I have never seen it in Europe. Finally, if you need a last minute gift for a woman, flowers are readily available on major street-corners, and are rather inexpensive. Oh, yes, if you plan to take alcohol or tobacco for gifts or for personal use, make sure you know what the customs limits are. Your airline and the guidebooks can help you with this.

Packing each container

Here is a checklist for the distribution of items in each of the "containers" described in the body of this chapter. This list is not intended to be definitive. It is merely a guideline to help you avoid forgetting or misplacing something important.

1. The suitcase
   - ☐ clothing
   - ☐ second pair of shoes (optional)
   - ☐ empty nylon bag
   - ☐ electrically powered grooming aids (if you must)
   - ☐ soap
   - ☐ washcloth
   - ☐ talcum or foot powder
   - ☐ spare camera film
   - ☐ extra batteries
   - ☐ suntan oil
   - ☐ alcohol towelettes
   - ☐ facial tissues
   - ☐ sewing kit
   - ☐ first aid kit
   - ☐ plastic bags
   - ☐ toilet paper
   - ☐ rubber bands
   - ☐ crazy glue
   - ☐ flashlight
   - ☐ gifts
   - ☐ car and house keys
   - ☐ alarm clock
   - ☐ corkscrew
   - ☐ plastic cups
   - ☐ bottle opener
   - ☐ nylon cooler bag
   - ☐ audio tapes (optional)

- ☐ jewelry (if you must)
- ☐ matches or lighter
- ☐ purse with U.S. coins
- ☐ spare prescription

2. The purse or briefcase
   - ☐ minimal grooming materials
   - ☐ poncho or umbrella
   - ☐ camera
   - ☐ film
   - ☐ prescription medications
   - ☐ non-prescription medications
     - ☐ aspirin
     - ☐ sleeping pills
     - ☐ medication for diarrhea
   - ☐ inflatable neck pillow
   - ☐ set of underclothing
   - ☐ things that would set off the airport x-ray machine
   - ☐ reading material
   - ☐ guidebooks
   - ☐ maps
   - ☐ compass
   - ☐ slippers (optional)
   - ☐ power converter
   - ☐ batteries
   - ☐ notebook
   - ☐ postcard addresses
   - ☐ genealogical reference material
   - ☐ spare ballpoint pen
   - ☐ spare prescription glasses
   - ☐ sun glasses
   - ☐ other breakable items
   - ☐ copies of your vital documents
     - ☐ credit and ATM cards
     - ☐ passport
     - ☐ frequent flier identification number
     - ☐ critical phone numbers

- ☐ drivers license number
- ☐ international drivers license
- ☐ prescriptions for medication
- ☐ travelers check numbers
- ☐ rental contracts
- ☐ airline tickets
- ☐ train tickets

3. The nylon bag
   - ☐ nothing (save it for dirty laundry and/or purchases)

4. The security wallet
   - ☐ passport
   - ☐ credit and ATM cards
   - ☐ travelers checks
   - ☐ drivers license
   - ☐ international drivers license
   - ☐ cash in excess of $100

5. Your body
   - ☐ coat
   - ☐ sweater
   - ☐ walking shoes
   - ☐ ballpoint pen
   - ☐ airplane tickets
   - ☐ wallet
     - ☐ small U.S. bills
     - ☐ $100 of foreign currency
     - ☐ one travelers check
   - ☐ purse for foreign coins
   - ☐ pocket knife

6. Leave these at home
   - ☐ bulky items
   - ☐ electrically-powered grooming aids
   - ☐ notebook computer
   - ☐ jewelry

- ☐ video camera
- ☐ the dog
- ☐ the kids

Chapter 4
Flight Arrangements

We're off!
So what's the big deal? All you have to do is buy a ticket and get on the plane. Right? Wrong! The first significant step on your great European adventure is when you go to the airport to board the plane — either the flight to Europe, or a connecting flight if you live off the beaten track like us. That first step can be a delightful start for your trip, or it could set you off on the wrong foot, or it could even be the end of your trip. Let's go through the flight a step at a time to make sure you have it right.

Which airline?
How do you go about choosing an airline? You can choose from United, American, Continental, TWA, Air France, Swissair, KLM, British Airways, and a number of others. Ask your traveling acquaintances which airlines they prefer, and why. Ask travel agents the same questions. And check prices, repeatedly. When you have decided on an airline, you will want to stick with it. The major airlines have mileage programs where you gain credit for future trips. Sometimes an airline will offer a credit card that brings with it a bonus,

such as a free ticket for a companion traveler. We have been fortunate in experiencing both of these advantages. They radically reduce the single biggest expense of your trip, the airline tickets.

Airline to where?

One of the factors that you want to consider is what cities these airlines serve. For example, on one airline you can get to Frankfurt, Germany, but not to Munich without an expensive connecting flight. On another airline you can get to Milan, Italy but not to Florence or Rome. There are three different international airports in Paris, France. If you are going to the south of France, you might not want to land at De Gaulle airport to the north of the city. Just like all of your decisions in planning a trip, you are faced with choices.

One of the factors that we have taken into account is the rental of a car on the other end of the flight. Car rentals are least expensive in Spain, inexpensive in Germany, more expensive in France, and most expensive in Italy. The rental agencies in some countries ban the use of their cars in some other countries. They forbid taking their cars to Eastern Europe. They forbid taking expensive cars to Italy. In England they require purchase of special insurance if you are taking the car abroad, even to Ireland. Generally, if you stay within the European Economic Community, and if you stay away from luxury cars, you are free to cross borders with no concern. Since the car rental is your second largest expense item, you will want to explore the alternatives as a part of choosing the European airport to which you want to fly.

One thing to think about a bit is where your seats are on the plane. Some people, like Nancy, prefer a window seat. Some people, like me, prefer an aisle seat. It works out well for us that way. John and Margie prefer aisle seats across from one another. Some people prefer a row with an emergency exit. No, they are not paranoid. They have learned that such rows usually provide more leg room. What nobody wants, if they can avoid it, is a seat in the middle of a set of three or four. Whatever your seat preference, try to obtain it at the same time that you make your reservations.

Buying the ticket

There are better and worse times to buy a ticket. If you delay too long, you can find that the flights you want are filled. We commit to our flights in the middle of January. At that time there are plenty of seats. We always deal with the (800) telephone number of our selected airline. We ask if there are any special discounts – for advantage card holders, for senior citizens, or for any other reason. We always look for coach class tickets, since they are only a fraction of the price of business class and – God forbid – first class tickets.

Then we call the same (800) number two or three more times with the same questions. It is amazing how inconsistent the answers are. The pricing systems of the airlines are so complicated that it is difficult for a ticket agent to sort out the options. When we hear a price that seems to be the lowest we are likely to get, we make our decision and reserve our tickets while still on the phone. It is sort of like a Dutch auction where the asking price keeps coming down until someone makes a bid. After we have made the reservation, we have from one to three days to pay for the tickets. Usually we pay for them with a credit card while we are still on the phone.

That is not the end of the price negotiations. If you ask, the ticket agent will confirm several things that prevent your ticket purchase from being an absolutely final commitment. If there is an illness or a death in the family, you can obtain a refund on your tickets for a modest fee. If the price of tickets drops, you can go back to the airport and either turn in your ticket for another at the lower price, or alternatively, obtain a refund of the difference. The refund is usually in the form of a voucher to be used to help purchase future flights.

Our experience has been that ticket prices are often reduced in the March and April time frame. One year we obtained three different price reductions – to about two-thirds of the original purchase price. Seems like a lot of trouble? Not really. If we had waited until March or April, we might not have found room on the flights we preferred.

Verify your flights

When you have your tickets in hand, read them to verify that the price and the schedule of the flights are what you expected them to be. There have been people who have had nasty surprises at the departure gate because they neglected to read the tickets when they arrived. If you buy your tickets early like we do, you might find that the airline has changed the flight schedule by the time you are ready to leave. If so, they are supposed to (read *supposed to*) notify you. It is prudent to telephone the airline about two weeks before departure to verify the schedule. The whole schedule.

Check-in

The airline wants you to check in about two hours before a transatlantic flight. There is usually no problem if you arrive at the check-in desk no later than an hour before your flight. But, there are some very good reasons to check in earlier. First of all, if you forgot your tickets, or your drivers license, or other photo identification, you might still have time to correct the error. However, if you made that error, who knows what other important thing you forgot. Maybe you should stay at home.

The check-in desk we are talking about here is the one where you leave the luggage that you don't want to carry with you on the plane. If you packed as was advised in the previous chapter, you really don't have to check in your luggage if you don't want to. The down side of carrying all of your luggage on the plane is that if you don't live near an international airport, you have to carry it between flights. The up side is that you can be assured that your luggage won't be lost en route, and you won't have to wait for the airport to deliver it to the carousel when you arrive.

All of this might soon become passé. The airlines are finding that more and more passengers are using the smaller "stewardess" suitcases and are carrying them on the plane. Storage room in the cabin is limited. Soon the airlines might be forced to restrict carry-on luggage.

The bomb in the suitcase

We were on a trip to France. Nancy had packed some presents for friends. One was a beautiful crystal piece, holding a battery-powered clock. It was to be a gift for some newlyweds. As a conscientious gift-bearer, Nancy installed the battery and set the clock. She then put the package into the center of her suitcase to protect it from damage.

As we passed through the x-ray machine at the airport, the operator did a double take and immediately called for her supervisor. It did not take long to demonstrate that Nancy was not a bomb-carrying terrorist. The chuckles we shared with the airport staff almost made up for the disarrangement of the things she had packed so carefully.

This was as humorous as the time when an x-ray operator thought that the cane-handled umbrella in my briefcase was a gun. Or the time when I was returning from Paris with a plaster gargoyle for our son. The x-ray operator must have thought he had found a plastic bomb. I regret that I didn't have a camera to capture his expression when he unwrapped the package.

Departure gate

The second check-in is at your gate of departure. If you decide to carry your own luggage, you could skip the first check-in desk. This second desk is where you can enter the great ticket lottery. Read on.

There is a very important reason why we check in for our flights early. Because we have a flexible schedule in Europe, we are in a position to accept a bump if it is offered. You don't know what a bump is? It is a delay to a later flight in exchange for a free ticket for your next flight to Europe. Since empty seats are lost revenue, and since some passengers cancel their reservations at the last minute, airlines customarily sell more tickets than they have seats. Some of the passengers have tickets, but not seats. If, however, the cancellations are fewer than expected, the airline will announce an offer of compensation for passengers who accept a bump to a later flight. On overseas flights it is not uncommon for people to be reluctant to accept a bump, since they are eager to reach their destination and are usually operating on a tight personal schedule. When we check in early for our flight, we always ask how full the plane is, and offer to accept a bump — depending upon the terms offered. This has worked about one flight in ten.

There is one inconvenience in accepting a bump. If your luggage has been checked in, it will arrive at your destination before you. No real problem. It will be at the unclaimed luggage desk when you arrive. The only serious inconvenience is if you arrive after the unclaimed luggage desk has closed. Then you will have to spend the night near the airport in order to pick up your luggage the next day.

Bumps also work on return flights. Weekend flights are the most likely to be over-booked. Although tickets cost a modest premium for weekend flights, we usually prefer them. It is a lottery with a good expected return. The typical compensation for a transatlantic bump is in the form of a $700 travel voucher that can be used to buy next year's ticket. Once we accepted bumps for two days in a row when returning from Paris. Our food and lodging were paid for by the airline at a fine hotel near the airport. We had a free weekend in Paris, and came home with two $700 vouchers apiece. Not bad. What with the price reductions on the tickets, an occasional free companion ticket, and the bumps, we joke about the possibility that the airline might pay us to patronize their competitors. They would save money!

At the check-in, if not before, the airline is likely to ask you for a phone number where you can be reached while in Europe. The reason for this is that they would like to inform you if the schedule for your return flight is changed. If you travel like us, you seldom know where you will be on a given day, and have no phone number to give them. Your alternative is to ask the ticket agent for the phone number of the airline in the city from which you will come home. That way you can phone them a day or two before your planned return to verify your flight schedule.

On the plane

What do you do on the plane? Sit and wait. It certainly is a long trip, usually about seven to nine hours. For this reason the airlines and experienced travelers have developed a number of techniques for passing the time.

The airline tries to keep you occupied. On one flight Nancy counted eleven different times that the stewardesses approached us. They offered complimentary newspapers and magazines. They offered free cocktails. They distributed hot towels before dinner. They served dinner. They served drinks with dinner. They served after-dinner drinks and coffee. And sold duty-free items. And orange juice in the morning. And breakfast. And an extra coffee after breakfast. And, finally, landing cards so that we could tell the customs officials that we weren't bringing anything illegal into the country.

Our technique is to make ourselves as comfortable as possible, and to try to sleep as much as possible. The free drinks help somewhat if you don't overdo it. I find that my best results come if I put on the earphones (also free on international flights) and select a channel of mellow music, preferably classical. I then watch the movie that is shown about an hour after dinner. A movie without sound soon becomes incredibly dull. That is usually good for a few hours of sleep.

How to make yourself comfortable? As I said before, Nancy likes a window seat. Comfort is one reason. When it is too dark to look out the window, she leans against the bulkhead and closes her eyes. Some people carry slippers, and blinders to keep out the light. But everybody sits, and sits, and sits. If you can sleep, all the better. If you can't sleep, a good travel companion and a good book can work wonders to pass the time. If you carry this specific book with you, you can learn interesting things, or maybe you can be bored into a sound sleep!

One more comfort technique. If you are awake about an hour and a half before arrival, make use of the toilet. In addition to making room for your morning coffee, you might want to freshen up. It is amazing how much better you feel. Remember that disposable razor you packed in your briefcase? The best thing is that you have just managed to beat the rush. When orange juice is being served, the lines for use of the facilities become very long.

No rest for the wicked

John and Margie were on their way to Africa for a photo safari. (This doesn't all have to be about Europe, does it?) The flight was to last more than twelve hours. John noticed that the rear of the plane had many empty seats. He moved back to a row of four empty seats, stretched out, and promptly fell asleep. A man tapped him on the shoulder and claimed they were his seats, all of them. The stewardess verified this, saying that the man had been given the seats to make up for being bumped from first class.

John moved to a set of three seats. A young lady was lying in two of them. She kept kicking John and said that she was embarrassed, since she had never slept with a man before.

John moved again. Soon the steward came to tell the two men in front of him to stop doing what they were doing under a blanket. "We don't operate that sort of airline." Finally, John returned to his own seat where two Mormon missionaries struck up a conversation with him. He says that he enjoyed the chat, but never did get any sleep.

Customs

That landing card that you fill out on the plane will be given to the person at the passport check in your airport of arrival. If you aren't a criminal, and if you aren't carrying illegal substances, don't worry. It is a formality. Usually, the only question you are asked is whether you are traveling on business or for pleasure. Sometimes you are also asked how long you plan to stay. Then the nice young man or woman will put a visa stamp on a page of your passport.

From the passport desk you will go to pick up your check-in luggage, if any. Then you will pass by the customs desk. Agents are there to confirm that you aren't carrying anything illegal. Drugs are illegal. Too much tobacco is illegal. Too much liquor is illegal. Even too much money (very much money) is illegal. If you plan to carry more that one bottle of liquor or more than enough tobacco for your personal use, ask the airline – before you pack your luggage – what the limits are for your destination country.

What do you do if your luggage is lost, God forbid, or if it is delayed, or if the luggage pickup area is closed. The first thing that you do is say a few unsavory words. Now that you have relieved the tension, you go to the office that traces lost luggage. They will help you fill out a form describing the luggage and telling what flight you were on. They will want to know where to deliver the luggage when it is found. If you are on a driving tour like us, obtain the phone number of the office so that you can call them. Oh yes, always remember that if your trip involved several airlines, the one that delivered you to your final destination is responsible for the recovery of your luggage. Or payment for the loss.

You will find a red sign and a green sign where you leave the luggage pickup area. If you follow the green sign, you won't be bothered by a customs agent. If you think you might be carrying something questionable, follow the red sign and be prepared for a minor inconvenience as your luggage is searched. What you don't ever want to do is to follow the green sign when you are carrying something you shouldn't have.

The two-fisted drinker

I was on a business trip to Europe. I was carrying a bottle of scotch and one of bourbon as gifts for friends who would no doubt entertain me for dinner. As the plane was approaching Paris, I noticed in the flight magazine that France allowed the entry of only one liter of alcohol per person.

So, like a good visitor, I chose the red sign line as I left the luggage area. There were two customs officers seated behind a small table. I approached them, and said in my best (not good) French, "J'ai deux bouteilles." Or, "I have two bottles." The response was a laconic, "De quoi?" or, "Of what?" I said, "Whiskey." The response to that was a classic Gallic shrug and a wave of the hand that clearly said, "Go away, and don't bother us with trivia."

Jet lag

Well, you did it. You survived the trip. Tired, but undaunted, you are ready to meet the Old World. Wait a minute. Count up the hours of sleep that you had – or didn't have. You can expect to experience jet lag for a day or two. How do you deal with it?

The worst thing you can do is to try to take a nap in bed during your first afternoon in Europe. Your body will think it is night and will sleep a lot longer than you intend it to. After all the clock says that it is early in the morning, but your body thinks it should be midnight. Then it will wake up in the middle of the night (it is really day to your body) and be ready to conquer the world. If you thought the flight was long, spare yourself an even longer night of insomnia.

The technique that seems best for us is to keep on the move during our first day in Europe. A quick catnap in the car is all right so long as a travel companion makes sure you don't nap for more than an hour at a time. If you keep moving, you can then go to bed a bit earlier than usual the first night. If you are fortunate, you will sleep all night and be virtually free of jet lag by the next morning. But if you aren't that fortunate, don't feel too bad. Some people adjust quickly, others slowly. It seems that some biological clocks are harder to reset than others.

How do you know when you are over jet lag? It is simple. You are over jet lag when your daily bodily functions take place at the usual time. Do I need to be more specific? and indelicate?

Chapter 5
Renting a Car

Selecting an agency

Renting a car in Europe isn't essentially different from renting a car in the U.S. Unless you have a local contact with a low-price, reliable agency, you are best advised to do business with one of the major car rental agencies. Consider names such as Avis, Hertz, Alamo, Budget, and Europcar. They all have (800) telephone numbers. You want to ask for the desk that handles foreign rentals. You might also want to verify if the agency gives air mileage credit for your rental, or if it gives a discount because you bought your tickets from a specific airline.

The car rental agencies establish a new annual rate schedule about the middle of January each year. Unlike the airlines, they rarely seem to be sold out. You could delay making your car reservation if you wish.

One time we had very poor service from the Budget desk at Orly airport. Other than that, we have always found good to excellent service from all of the major agencies. For that reason, I suggest that you base your choice of agency solely on price. You must be careful about price, however. It might or might not include all of the following items. Ask the agent on the telephone to clarify.

- basic daily or weekly rate,
- insurance, unless you reject it,
- airport tax (usually paid at the airport,)
- pickup charge (usually paid at the airport,)
- drop-off charge
- charge for any additional driver (usually paid at the airport,) and
- value added tax, currently 12% to 21%.

Generally, you can save money by paying in advance for your car by credit card when you make the reservation for it. If something causes you to change your plans, you can cancel your reservation without charge, even up to a day or two before the time you are to pick up the car.

Crossing borders

If you are planning to visit other countries than the one in which you are renting your car, check with the agent to see if there are restrictions on where you can take it. The Eastern block countries are still in economic and political turmoil to some extent. For that reason it is not uncommon for the agency to tell you that you cannot take their car there. If you are renting an expensive car, you might be told that you can't take it to Italy, where there is more than the usual amount of car theft. If you are traveling to Italy or Hungary – both of them great tourist sites – plan to rent your car there.

When you do drive across national boarders, be prepared to stop for a passport check if you are going in or out of the European Economic Community. If you are passing between countries that are in the EEC, drive slowly, and don't be surprised if you are totally ignored. The border guard is often noted by its absence.

Selecting a car

European cars are generally a bit smaller than their U.S. counterparts, even if they are manufactured by a U.S. company. As in the U.S., don't expect to receive a car that is identical to the one you select. When the agent says your car will be a Ford Escort or the equivalent, you are likely to find yourself with the equivalent. This is no problem unless you have a brand fetish. The major concern you should have with your car is trunk space. Discuss this with the agent if you aren't confident about the capacity of the models that interest you. We have found that class B cars, like the Ford Escort or the Volkswagon Golf are just right for us, whether there are two or four people in our party. If you don't pack compactly as advised in Chapter 3, then you would do well to rent a larger car.

There are a few other things about European cars that differ from U.S. cars. At least 90% of cars are built with a manual transmission. If you can't handle a stick, make sure to order a car with an automatic transmission. And expect to pay extra for it. Only a limited percentage of cars have air conditioning. Hot weather is not as common in Europe as it is here. If you insist on air conditioning, it will cost extra. If you don't specifically ask for it, you probably won't get it.

A large percentage of cars have diesel engines. The only inconvenience is a fraction of a minute wait for the engine to warm up when you start it. Diesel engines are more economical to operate than gasoline engines. This is a distinct advantage in Europe where fuel is four or five times as expensive as in the U.S. Remember, that the "reasonable" price you see on the gas pump is not the price of a gallon, but the price of a liter, which is only slightly more than a quart.

One more thought about the size of your car. Unless you are convinced that you must have a "full sized" car, rent a small one. Many of the roads and streets in Europe date from medieval times, if not from Roman times. They tend to be rather narrow. You might be tempted to rent a van for a group of people. This is not necessarily a good idea unless your group is large and has a shortage of drivers. One van costs more than two cars. The van has another disadvantage. Your luggage is visible to anyone who passes by when you are parked.

The advantage of folding mirrors

Nancy and I were celebrating our 40th wedding anniversary. We had rented a farmhouse in Provence, a quaint and colorful area of France that is just north of the Mediterranean coast. We had invited our children to join us. Some were able to do so. To handle the "crowd," I rented a van.

We were in a modest-sized town on a Sunday morning looking for a church so that we could attend Mass. Churches in such towns tend to be in the old, medieval area. Narrow streets you know. I found the church finally, after several false turns. One of these was a short journey down a side street that gradually narrowed so that both of the side-view mirrors folded back against the windows. Better the mirrors than the fenders.

Added features
Your car will almost certainly be equipped with a radio. A tape player is less likely to be included, but is becoming more common, especially in larger cars. We always carry a few tapes just in case.

Your car might have a novel feature. Look for a pocket in the doors that is made to hold a bottle of water. Although tap water is quite drinkable in almost all of western Europe, bottled water has become the style – much more so than here. People almost always order bottled water with a meal, even though tap water is available without charge. Because of the lack of air conditioning in cars, it is often convenient to carry a bottle to refresh yourself on the road. It is also convenient for cleaning up after a roadside picnic.

Rental desk
When you arrive at your destination airport, look for the car rental desks. They will be located near the luggage pickup carousels just as in the U.S. The paperwork at the desk will be only a little more detailed than what you are accustomed to. The clerk will have a sufficient knowledge of English to handle the transaction with no great difficulty. You will need to show your drivers license, a credit card, and your passport.

The rental agent will ask if you wish to take out insurance, and will probably even recommend it. We have always found that we can obtain adequate insurance in advance, either from our own insurance agent, or as an adjunct – often free – of our credit card or airline ticket.

Ed and I both had experience with damaged cars. He once was broadsided within a minute of leaving the Hertz garage in Brussels. They immediately gave him a replacement car. We had a car that was badly damaged by hail the day before we returned it in Paris. Hertz was quite understanding, and shrugged it off as an act of God.

Sometimes, even though you paid in advance, you will probably face extra charges for airport tax, road tax, pickup charge, and extra drivers. Keep a copy of all paperwork. If you provide a copy of the documents to the main office of the rental agency on your return, you will receive a prompt and courteous refund if you were overcharged. They understand the difficulty of communicating between continents.

Oh yes, one more thing before you leave the rental desk at the airport. Ask them for a map of the area and a map of the country. These maps are free. Have the agent show you on the area map how to get to the first major highway that you plan to use.

Picking up the car

When you pick up your car, be sure to examine it for any significant damage. Small dents and scrapes don't count. Have the rental agent make a note of the dents or scratches. If you return a car with significant damage, the assumption will be made that you caused it by an accident. If you do have an accident, the rental agency will want you to report it to their nearest office within 40 hours.

If you are like us, you are in a hurry to get in the car and be on your way. Wait a minute longer. Ask the rental agent to show you anything unusual about the car. That will be difficult, since nothing about the car will be unusual to the agent, only to you. Verify how to honk the horn. On some cars you tap on the end of the gearshift lever to operate the horn. Ask if the car has an anti-theft alarm, and how to turn it on and off. Make sure you can find reverse gear. On some cars you must depress the gearshift as you move it to the reverse position. Verify what sort of fuel the car uses. By the time you ask all of these questions, the agent will know that you are a novice at this. He might even tear up the contract and tell you to rent from someone else. Not really.

Once we picked up our car in an underground garage that was crowded and dimly lit. Being in a hurry to get on with the journey, I failed to take the time to examine the car in the light as we left the garage. The fact that it was raining added to my reluctance. Sure enough, when we arrived at our first night's destination, I found a long cut in one door. It looked as if the car had brushed against a sharp rock. We had only stopped once on that day's trip, parking in a lot with many other cars. I photographed the damage and had the agent make a note of the problem on the contract when I returned the car several weeks later. About a month after returning home, I received a letter from the agency asking me to fill out a form to describe the "accident." I sent a letter back, without their form, explaining the circumstances. I also enclosed a copy of the photo and of the contract with the note written by their agent. No further correspondence was needed.

Where is M-VI?

We had arrived at the Madrid airport. It was quite a hassle, since we had come from three different places. I arrived first by train from Paris after celebrating a family reunion in Luxembourg. Nancy came next from Illinois and wasn't far behind schedule. Jack and June were coming from Phoenix and had been delayed four hours by a tornado in Dallas. But, anyway, we were all there and ready to get on the road.

I asked the car rental agent to show me how to get on the highway for Salamanca, to the west of Madrid. He showed me how to get to M-40, the beltline expressway. He then said to take the exit for M-VI and A6, which would take us to Salamanca. We soon passed exits for M-I and M-II, saw signs that more M-exits were coming up, and then came to an exit for A6. Three people said to take that exit. I, the navigator, said to drive on and wait for M-VI. Wrong. The M-VI signs had never been installed.

When it finally dawned on the navigator what had happened, we were to the south of Madrid. To heck with it. We took the road to Toledo. A great choice! Some day we might go back to Salamanca.

Leaving the airport

Ok, you have your car. You are ready to get on the road. You are eager to be off on your great adventure. Wait a minute! To avoid needless problems, take care of one last minute item.

Drive around the airport, and learn to recognize the signs and the roads you will use to return the car when you are done with it. It is always difficult for me to comprehend the signs and conventions in domestic airports. European airports are at least as confusing. If you are going to get lost, do so on your first day, not when you are rushing to catch your flight home. One last thing to check. If you plan to return the car with a full fuel tank (a good economy measure,) look for a service station near the airport, and then remember where it is.

Chapter 6
Driving

Expect the unexpected

Remember Murphy's law? It says something to the effect that if something can go wrong, it will. Then there is O'Toole's Rule. It says that Murphy is an optimist. Both apply to driving in a foreign country. Although there might be little danger of anything serious happening, there are innumerable small things that seem to go wrong. If, like me, you like to tell stories, driving will give you abundant material. That is why this chapter has more than its share of anecdotes.

Right hand drive

Everyone has heard about the difficulty of driving in Great Britain where the steering wheel is on the right side of the car, and people drive on the left hand side of the road. Really it is not bad as long as you concentrate on what you are doing, and no emergency develops. I remember a friend who was driving there for the first time and came upon a traffic situation that called for a quick change of gears. He jammed his hand against the lever – and wrapped the turn signal around the steering post.

Ed and April recommend renting a car at the airport and driving country roads until you are comfortable with the conventions. That makes sense to me, even though my experience would tend to be different.

I began my first drive in downtown London. It seemed to be no problem, since all I had to do was follow the traffic. However, we went on a trip to Cambridge. On the way back we were on an expressway (carriageway) with three lanes in each direction. I moved to the left hand lane so people could pass me on the right. There was a concrete curb at the left edge of the lane. I forgot that I was in England, and drifted a bit to the left so that I was looking down the road just to the left of center, as I do at home. I should have been to the right of center. I was quick to realize this when the hubcaps self-destructed as they scraped the curb.

The most serious, and insidious, challenge is to remember which way to look as you cross a street or enter an intersection, either in a car or on foot. Our instinctive reflex is to look to the left for oncoming traffic. In the United Kingdom that traffic will be coming from the right. I personally have another instinct that keeps Jack on edge and watching. If I am turning onto a road with a lane separation, I automatically go to the right of it. Wrong!

Reading maps

There are several companies that provide excellent maps of European countries. They come in a broad price range and in a variety of scales. The ones we like best are published by Michelin. They are quite similar to the type you can buy in a gas station or book shop at home. The significant difference, and a disappointing one, is that they don't contain an index showing the coordinates of cities and towns, or a table showing the mileage between major cities. One nice thing, however, is that they show the meaning of map symbols in several major languages, including English. Another nice thing is that they have symbols showing the location of castles, ancient ruins, prehistoric sites, and scenic views. The names of parks, caves and other natural attractions are highlighted by a colored rectangle. Cities, towns and villages that are of interest to tourists are marked on the maps with a star. As you plan your itinerary, look at the routes you will travel and note the possible side trips of an hour to a day, depending on how charmed you are when you reach the star with your car. There now, doesn't that make you eager to get on with your first trip?

A map of the scale of 1:1,000,000 to 1:2,000,000 is quite adequate for traveling on major roads. You will also want to buy small-scale maps on the order of 1:200,000 for any area that you want to explore by using local roads. These maps even show you the shape of towns and villages. If you go far from a major road without the aid of a small-scale map, you can be certain of getting lost. Remember, almost all of the roads follow old cow paths. If you find that you need a number of these small-scale maps, then you might consider buying a book of detailed maps for your target country. They run from $10 to $15 – a bargain. Even if you buy such a book, you will find the large scale map of the country handy to give you a perspective. When Jack is driving and I am navigating with a small-scale map, he will ask, "Where are we?" I will say that we are about 5 km. from such-and-such a village. His response is, "That's fine, but where are we?" He is more comfortable if he knows where the village is in respect to the rest of the country.

When you need to drive in a major city, you will want to obtain a map of that city. They are available at tourist offices, book stores and gas stations. If you go to a tourist office, or to the concierge at a hotel, they will be free. The tourist office is most often located in or adjacent to the major railroad stations. Just follow the tracks.

Tollway traps

Tollways in the U.S. are always a challenge for the uninitiated. There are even more surprises to be had in Europe. You would do well to accept this as just another interesting challenge. The following three stories illustrate this.

Portuguese conventions

It is fortunate that tollways are inexpensive in Portugal. There are a few local conventions that can get you into trouble. You pick up a ticket when you enter the tollway. Then, when you leave, the attendant at the exit gate uses the ticket to determine what you have to pay.

Once we stopped at a rest stop on a tollway to spend the night in a motel. A sign behind the reception desk cautioned guests to obtain a special receipt when checking out, for the purpose of avoiding extra toll. Naturally I forgot. When I turned in my ticket on leaving the tollway, the clerk asked for my receipt. She apologized and smiled when she had to charge me extra for "using the tollway overnight."

On the same tollway, I didn't read the signs carefully at the tollgate where tickets are issued. So, I breezed through a no-stop gate intended for those who have passes. As I left the tollway, I used much arm waving to explain to the toll clerk what had happened. She too smiled and shrugged as she charged me the full toll from the far end of the tollway. Nancy says that we learn from our mistakes. I must be learning a lot.

Where did you come from?

Jerry and Mary were on the expressway heading away from Paris to explore the French countryside. They came to a toll booth where they were to pick up a ticket that would determine what they were to pay when they exited the expressway. As they sat at the booth deciphering the signs, a large Volvo truck pulled up behind them. The driver became impatient and blew his horn – a very loud horn. Jerry quickly pulled out into traffic, wondering what he had missed.

He found out when he went to leave the expressway. The clerk asked for the ticket. No ticket. Where did you get on the expressway? Paris. Why no ticket? Language, impolite truck driver, loud horn. The clerk was kind and gave them the benefit of the doubt. The chuckles that come from within Jerry as he tells the story more than repay him for the momentary inconvenience.

Full service toll booths

We were driving on the expressway east of Paris. We came to the first tool booth. I reached into my wallet and pulled out a hundred franc note. Nancy had found several such banknotes in our travel supplies when we packed for the trip. I put them into my wallet without looking at them.

It took an unusually long time for the clerk to give me the change – at least 30 seconds. Slow for a toll clerk. The change was just a few coins. As I drove off, I looked at the coins in my hand and began to wonder if I had been short-changed. Then it dawned on me. The banknote was one from Belgium where the franc is about 20% of the value of a French franc. The delay was the time it took for the toll clerk to look up the appropriate exchange rate.

Can you imagine what would happen in the U.S. if you gave a foreign banknote to a toll clerk?

Speed limits

Unless specifically marked as an exception, speed limits are rather consistent. The famous Autobahn in Germany has no speed limit other than what your car can accomplish. The expressway limit in France is 130 km. per hour, or about 80 mph. In Spain and Portugal it is 120 km. per hour. The limit on two lane roads in the countryside is 90 kph, or about 55 mph. The limit within cities and villages is 50 kph, or about 35 mph. Be careful in Ireland, which is in the process of converting to the metric system. At the time of this writing speed limits are posted in miles per hour, while distances are posted in kilometers.

Your natural instincts and the power limitations of your car will generally keep you out of trouble with speed limits. On the expressway you will be traveling a lot faster than you are accustomed to at home. Besides, in Europe most people travel from 10 to 20 kph faster than the limit, seemingly without unduly disturbing the law enforcement authorities. And again, your car, if a class B like we rent, won't operate quietly above 130 kph. On country roads, you are traveling at the same relative speed as at home. In town you will be traveling at your normal speed unless you have a lead foot. Town streets are often narrow, with the houses placed close to the street. You should be uncomfortable at any speed above the limit. In any case, the old rule of thumb applies. If you are traveling with the mass of traffic, you are in no danger of being stopped for speeding.

Although you can make better time when you drive on expressways, you might want to save that for long distance travel. You don't see as much of the country on an expressway. And in some countries, such as in France, the tolls are not insignificant. In Germany, Luxembourg and the U.K. the expressways are free. In Portugal they are inexpensive. In Spain they are generally free, but the few tollways are relatively inexpensive .

If you are stopped on the highway by police, don't panic. In this case, your limited ability or lack of ability with the local language can be an asset to you. The police in Europe are a bit more inclined to stop traffic if they are searching for specific lawbreakers. They are polite and even friendly. They will soon have you back on your way. But take note! Don't panic! Police in Europe, particularly those on a highway stakeout, often carry submachine guns. It is a bit of a shock to face a very young man with peach fuzz cheeks, carrying a submachine gun at the ready. This is just one more local custom to accept as different from yours.

If you see a pair of policemen alongside the road and they aren't carrying guns, don't worry about them. Usually they are looking for cars with outdated licenses. Even if they stop you, which they almost certainly won't, the problem will be the rental agency's, not yours. In Spain they might be looking for proof that you are adequately insured. In this case any failure is your problem – a $500 problem.

Driving conventions

There are a few differences in driving conventions that you would do well to be aware of. No problem if you are forewarned. A possible inconvenience or even an accident if you are not mentally prepared.

On an expressway some people travel significantly faster than the speed limit, particularly those who drive a Mercedes or a BMW. These cars are comfortable at speeds of 120 mph. I'm not comfortable, but the car is. One of these people at any moment will pull into the left lane to pass a slower car. It doesn't matter who is coming up in the left lane or at what speed they are coming. First out is first in line. Be prepared to touch the brakes occasionally when you are in the left lane and are passing someone at a reasonable speed. He might just pull out in front of you to pass a still slower car ahead of him. If you are in the passing lane and a speeder comes up behind you, he will ride your bumper and flash his lights at you – day or night. It depends on your temperament whether you thumb your nose at him or give him the right of way. Personally, I am always aware that I am a guest in that country.

In France there is a general rule that the person on the right has the right of way. It is called the "priority of the right." This is usually no problem, except during rush hours. Then people have been known to drive up on the sidewalk at a stoplight to get ahead of the other people in the proper lanes, who are now to the left. Every country has its share of discourteous nuts.

In Spain there is a great tendency to pass on two-lane roads. In order to avoid waiting for adequate room, the passer will cut in as soon as his rear bumper is in front of your front bumper. It is rather disconcerting. This in not the action of an overly aggressive driver, but a standard driving convention of the country. The Portuguese and the Irish have a different way of accomplishing the same trick. They pass on a two-lane road as if it were a three or four-lane road. The person coming toward you slides toward the side of the road. You are supposed to do the same on your side as you are passed. Wow! Not too bad once you learn the ropes.

The British started a roadway convention called the roundabout. The French call it a "rond-point" or round point. There are relatively few of these in the U.S. The roundabout is a way of providing access to several different, busy roads without resorting to stop signs or traffic lights. As you enter a roundabout, bear to the right (left in England) in the outside lane. The vehicles already in the outside lane have priority over you as you enter. When you come to a sign that indicates the road you want, possibly the continuation of the road from which you entered the roundabout, make a right (left in England) turn onto the highway. If you don't see the road you want, just continue around the roundabout another time or two until you are oriented. The persons in the inside lane are locals who know exactly where they are going, and why. They won't bother you unless you both head for the same exit at the same time. You might be honked at and cursed a bit by truck drivers, however. They don't seem to be as understanding as the average automobile driver.

If you don't see a sign for your road on your second or third trip around the roundabout, you have to make some sort of decision. We have learned that the odds are in your favor if you exit on the opposite side from where you entered. This is just one of many examples you will see where a road sign is absent at a place where you would think it logical to expect one. For lack of a sign, go straight ahead, but be prepared to do a U-ey. If you don't know what that is, read on.

The circus of Paris

Edouard is an old friend of ours who lives in Paris to the north of the Eiffel tower. In order to go to or from his apartment, he must travel past the Arch of Triumph. Eight streets meet at the great roundabout that circles the arch. The roundabout is about eight lanes wide, unmarked. There are so many accidents that the police don't bother to ask who was at fault. The drivers involved in an accident share the cost of repair equally.

When Edouard goes home from work he must travel around one-third of the roundabout. In that relatively short distance he always drives across all eight lanes to the center and then all the way back to the outside lane to his exit. It is a sporting affair with him. He never has an accident. The fact that he drives a large Jaguar might be a factor. Who wants to pay for half of the cost of repairing a Jaguar?

Once, early in the morning when traffic was very light I drove around the Arch. When we returned home I bragged about it to our younger daughter, Susie. In a somewhat supercilious tone she informed me that she had done the same during rush hour in a right-hand-drive station wagon full of people. Keeps me humble.

Traffic lights

It is a mistake to presume that you can make a right turn (left in England – tired of this yet?) at a red light. Laws on this vary. If nobody is honking and making obscene gestures at you from behind, it would be prudent to wait until the light turns green. Be careful to look for the stoplights. Some of them are tiny things on the side of buildings. A few of them are on the near side of an intersection. Thus, if you don't spot them in time, you will find that you are in front of the light and can't see when it turns green. Not a problem. If nobody is behind you, you can back up a bit. If somebody does pull up behind you, just wait until he honks at you.

The power of a U-ey

I have never been able to learn where and if U-turns are legal. But, if empirical evidence is to be believed, they are generally permitted. I know this because there have been many times that I made the wrong turn or missed a turn. It is very difficult in Europe to go "around the block" to correct for a wrong direction. Often there are no blocks, just roads meeting and branching in all directions. So, the only sure way of changing your direction quickly and accurately is to make a U-turn. We have done it so often that we refer to it as a "U-ey." We have never been arrested. Don't blame me, though, if it doesn't work for you. Oh yes, be sure you don't make a U-ey on a one-way street or on an expressway.

What country are we in?

We were on the way from Grenoble in the French Alps to Colmar in Alsace-Lorraine. There were two possible routes. The first, easier and slower, was to go west to Lyon, then north to Dijon and then northeast to Colmar. All in France. All on expressways. The shorter and faster route was to go east past Geneva, Switzerland, then north through the Black Forest region of Germany, then west across the Rhine to Colmar. Three countries, two languages, numerous routes, some of them not expressways – but shorter and faster.

We opted for the short route. Nearing the border between France and Switzerland, I turned onto the "logical" expressway. June, who never reads a map, said from the back seat, "You took the wrong turn." Sure enough. I had neglected to note that the continuation of the French expressway into Switzerland was identified by a different, Swiss, numbering system. I had looked for a route number. June had seen the sign pointing to Geneva. Now I had no idea what route we were on or what country we were in. It cost us about twenty minutes of time and a lot of good natured female-male abuse.

Signs

The road signs in Europe are generally very similar to those you are accustomed to. In fact, many of the icons on U.S. road signs are copied from those in Europe where half of any day's traffic past a point is from another country. The most important three signs are:

- the speed signs in kilometers per hour, not miles per hour (except in the U.K. and Ireland,)
- the no entry sign, which is round and red with a horizontal white bar, and
- the no parking sign, which is also round and red, but has a diagonal white bar going from lower left to upper right.

One sign on the expressways is a real treat. At home we have brown signs that tell of an interesting view or of an exit to a park. In Europe the brown signs have outline images of the things of interest, clusters of grapes, wild boars, castles, churches, and villages. The art techniques tend to vary by region. They are quite charming, and often humorous. Be sure to follow some of those that look interesting to you. What's your hurry?

Road and street signs are a bit different. On the highway, you often find your route by the name of a town or village that the road goes to. Yes, each road has a number, and yes, the number is printed on the road map. But no, the number is often missing from the highway sign that indicates the road. However, if you have found the right road, every once in a while you might see the route number displayed on short, very short, posts along the margin of the road. If you are looking for the route to city "A," the sign for the turn might not say "A,", but "B" or "C" which are other towns on the road between where you are and where "A" is, or even a long distance beyond the city that you are heading for. It is nice to have a good map reader in the seat alongside the driver. If the sign shows the names of a number of towns, the one on top is the furthest away, and the one on the bottom is the nearest. However, the sign is telling you that the road goes toward those towns, it does not guarantee that it goes to them. Be kind to your navigator.

In Spain and Portugal the conventions are like those in the U.S. Route numbers are more important than city names. That is, if there is any sign at all. And don't look for street signs in Portuguese cities. They are obvious by their absence. That is not much worse than the street signs in Belgium. Because there are two major linguistic groups in that country, all street signs are in both French and Flemish. Unfortunately, the two ethnic groups tend to dislike one another. So, you are apt to find one or both versions of a name on any sign painted over by a bigot from the other linguistic group. Consider it part of the great adventure.

If you have problems and get a little frustrated, count to ten. Go with the flow. This is one of the things that will make an entertaining story for your friends when you get home. If all else fails, stop and ask for directions. People are generally quite friendly and helpful. Of course, because of language difficulties (even in England – ever talk with a Cockney?) you might be given the wrong directions or might misunderstand. Start out on the indicated route. Stop soon and verify your directions with someone else.

The great chase scene

We had just had dinner in a nice restaurant in the old part of the city of Moulins in France. I was driving, and decided to take a different route out of town to our hotel in the countryside. It had rained during dinner, so the streets reflected our headlights and made it difficult to see clearly. The street became narrow, leaving me just enough room to drive through a space between two posts. I should have known better. I turned to the right, down a broader lane, and felt the front end of the car drop down a bump.

Three voices in unison urged me to stop. I had just driven the front end of the car down the first of a series of medieval steps. Fortunately they were shallow enough so that I was able to back up. As we left the area I wondered how it would have been if I had continued – like a chase scene in the movies. Nobody else seemed to be curious.

Into and out of town

No matter the size of the city or village, the way into and out of town is the same. And it is a lot simpler than in the U.S. As you come to a town you will see a sign saying "centre ville," or "zentrum," or any such word that means the center of town. Follow that sign and the series of similar signs until you have arrived. The heart of most cities is where the interesting things, the old things, are. You can't miss. Park the car in a convenient place, and wander.

When you leave, you have a different problem. How do you get back out of town, and on the right road? The problem seems insoluble until you have done it a few times – easily. Take any major street that seems to know where it is going. Sooner or later you will see a sign that says "toutes directions," or "alles richtungs," or anything else that seems to say "all directions." Follow that sign and any succeeding such signs. You are now on a belt-line that will take you past all of the major routes out of the city. Pick the one you want. Watch carefully. Unlike the roundabout, it will take a long time to recover if you miss your route. This is where a U-ey comes in handy.

In town

In a city the street signs take some getting used to. First of all, major streets have a habit of changing their names every mile or so. Before you grumble about "those crazy Europeans," try driving the main street of San Jose, California. It seems to change names every few blocks.

Sometimes the signs are missing. Sometimes, rarely, they are on signposts like our own street signs. Most of the time, however, they are cemented into the side of a corner building at the top of the first storey, our concept of a first storey that is. Read Chapter 8 to find out that European buildings do not number the floors in the same way that we do.

Probably my greatest problem with street signs is with the ones that are missing. This happens here at home, but seems to be more frequent in Europe. It is as if the street department of the local city assumes that since you are driving on the street, you already know the name of it. Wrong.

The larger the city, the harder it is to get around unless you are merely going to the center of town and then out again. The roads twist and turn. Up to eight streets might intersect at a single point. There are many one-way streets that are not indicated as such on the map. The first two times that Nancy and I drove in Paris we thought our marriage might be in jeopardy. But we survived and it survived. We learned the tricks. We learned from the school of hard knocks, fortunately not knocks on the car, but on our egos, which are more readily repaired. I might be at a red light. I would ask, "Which way do I turn?" The answer would be, "Wait until I find out where we are." Immediately upon the utterance of that last word the light would turn green, and the fellow behind us would honk his horn. I would make a quick decision, invariably wrong. I would then be asked, "Why didn't you wait?" This would be followed by, "You went the wrong way." This would in turn be followed by, "The streets aren't where the map says they are." My response will not be printed here. Obviously, we had to do something new. Here is the technique that we developed.

The first trick is to park the car, and walk or take public transportation. The larger the city, the better this advice is. If your trip begins or ends with several days in a large city, don't plan to rent a car for those days. There are two reasons why large European cities have excellent public transportation. The first is heavy traffic. The second is a shortage of parking. Sounds like Chicago to me.

The second trick is to look on the map in the area of the place you want to reach. Look for a major public building in that area. A railroad station, an opera house, a city hall, a palace, a cathedral, a monument, or any such thing now becomes your immediate goal. Go in the general direction of that goal, using major streets or what looks like a major street. Sooner or later you will see a sign that points to your intermediate goal. Only when you have reached that goal do you go back to the map, reading or trying to read street signs. It works like a charm – Paris, London (left, darn it,) Munich, Geneva, anywhere.

Hôtel de l'Ouest

Nancy and I were looking for the Hôtel de l'Ouest in the northwest corner of Paris. It was our first experience driving in the big city. The conversation quoted above took place that afternoon – many times. We were en route for several hours. This was also before we had learned the U-ey technique for quick recovery of direction.

Finally we noticed signs that pointed to a train station known as Gare St. Lazare. I remembered that the hotel was near the station. We reached it in ten minutes. No problem. Of course, the nearest garage was in a back alley several streets (not blocks) away. This took longer to reach. To vent my traffic frustration, I forced Nancy to go into the garage to negotiate space rental. I watched a great waving of hands through the window. She exited with a delightful smile. Her hands and her basic French had done the job. We didn't touch the ... car again until we left Paris.

Pedestrian rights

Read and remember this. It could be a matter of life or death for someone, including yourself. In most of Europe the pedestrian has the right of way when crossing the street at a marked crosswalk. This is similar to the conventions in California and Nevada. Your problem is that the local people have become quite accustomed to the convention, but many a tourist hasn't. Always give the person in a crosswalk the right of way. If a person is crossing outside a crosswalk, it would still be wise to give him the benefit of the doubt.

Parking in the Italian Tijuana

Nancy and I were on the Riviera. We learned that the Italian city, Ventimiglia, just across the border, had an open-air market on Fridays. We drove there. The traffic was heavy, but a policeman directed us down a lane to a parking area by the river. The lane was between stalls of goods for sale. Salespeople and customers readily backed out of our way as we slowly traversed the narrow lane.

A few years later we repeated the visit with Jack and June. I proudly showed off my foreign driving skill by starting down the lane once more. Jack went spastic, fearing that I would kill someone or at best pick up a traffic ticket. He had visions of rotting in an Italian jail. Not to fear. I know what I'm doing. Hah!

When I got to the end of the lane I learned that the parking area had been moved across the river. I was wondering why people seemed less willing to back out of my way.

Parking

In large cities, parking is like in Chicago, only worse. There aren't many parking spaces along the street, and what there are, are taken. Notice the occasional car with a boot on a left (right in England) wheel. Once you have a parking place, you tend to keep it. There are public and private lots. You pay for them. Oh yes, in most cities you pay for a parking space on the street if you happen to find one. Sometimes the meter won't take coins. Like everyone else, they are moving toward the use of plastic money. Fortunately the trend seems to be rather slow.

In major cities you are unlikely to find parking except in a public parking lot. Unfortunately there is a shortage of such lots. They are your best bet for safety when you do find one. Your rental car is less subject to damage there than it would be if you were to leave it on a narrow street. Besides, in Paris it is not uncommon for a person to park in too small a space. This is managed by banging and pushing the neighboring cars out of the way. Sort of like New York cab drivers.

In small towns parking is no problem. There are free public parking lots, and spaces in front of restaurants. The larger the community the more you find parking spaces to be dear – hard to find and sometimes expensive to pay for. Even major hotels and restaurants expect you to find your own parking somewhere else.

Parking lots (car parks in the U.K.)

If you are stopping at a hotel, park your car in the only free space you can find. You are probably legal for a few minutes. Run into the hotel and ask the concierge where the nearest parking garage is located. Have him draw you a map if he doesn't have one handy. At the garage you might have to pay in advance. Often you won't. After all, they have your car as insurance. You will usually be given a ticket that records when you parked. Don't leave it in the car. Put it in a pocket where you won't lose it. It will help you find your car again if you get lost. You will also want it in hand as you enter the parking area. You need it right away.

When you return to the garage for your car, look for a large machine by the doorway. It is there so you can pay your parking fee before you even get to your car. Put the ticket in the slot. The machine will read the ticket and will then display how much money you owe. Put in coins or bills until you have paid the amount shown on the machine. This is where that coin purse with lots of coins comes in handy. If you don't have enough coins or small bills, you might be able to get change from someone with limited patience or unlimited charity who is waiting in line behind you. Or you might get change from the garage attendant. Or you might have to go to a store or a bank. What you don't want to do is get into your car and approach the exit gate without having paid. When you have inserted the proper amount, the machine stamps your ticket. Take it with you.

The smaller machine at the exit gate will take your ticket, just like a machine at home. If you haven't paid the proper amount, a surly voice in an indecipherable language (indecipherable, even if you are reasonably fluent in the local language) will say unkind things to you. Of course if you stay where you are, an attendant will finally come and sort things out. They have seen lots of ignorant tourists.

The major underground parking deck in Luxembourg City is worth mentioning here. The Grand Duchy of Luxembourg is about the size of your county, with a population of less than 400,000 people. It is surrounded by France, Germany and Belgium. It has many tourists, and also has the best gasoline prices in Europe. The parking meter in the garage will take coins from five different countries. It even converts the rates to calculate how much more you need to deposit. Modern technology is wonderful!

Traffic jam at Orly

Nancy and I were on our first go-it-alone trip in France. We picked up the rental car with absolutely no problem and quickly followed the signs to the terminal where our luggage was waiting. We parked in the short term lot, picked up our luggage, and drove to the exit gate. There were barriers for about 50 meters, limiting the flow toward the gate to one car at a time.

At the gate was where I first learned that you pay your parking ticket in advance. By this time there were a number of cars behind me in the narrow lane. All of them had to back up to let me out so that I could pay my ticket. Nobody shot me, or cursed me, or even made an obscene gesture. Who ever said that Parisians are unfriendly?

By the way, I am a slow learner. I did the same thing a few years later at a parking lot near the Alhambra in Granada, Spain. There was a large tourist bus behind our car as I ran to the distant machine to pay my toll. The bus driver just smiled. He must have been earning overtime.

Fire!

We drove up to a hotel we had reserved in Paris. Naturally there was no parking lot. I parked on the street while Nancy went into the hotel to learn that we were to use a public garage "sort of around the corner." In the heart of Paris you can sometimes go around the block.

We found the garage and surrendered the car, which the attendant put someplace in the bowels of the earth.

The next morning we walked to the garage with our luggage, expecting to get on the road early. The garage was closed, and a wooden barrier was placed in front of the entry ramp right next to the sign that advertised 24 hour service. While we were standing there somewhat stupefied, another fellow came by and yelled down the drive. From the depths came a voice followed by a worn-looking man. He showed us to our cars. Water was dripping from the ceilings and running in the aisles. Black soot covered everything. During the night there had been a fire in the building above the garage. With a few paper towels we made it possible to see through the windows and left. There was no request or offer to pay the parking fee. Some day I should tell you about the problems involved in paying for and using tokens at an automatic car wash.

Street parking meters

On a European street you will not find meters like the ones you are accustomed to. If you wonder whether you need to pay for parking, look on the dashboards of a few neighboring cars. If they hold a small ticket, you pay. Somewhere along the sidewalk within 50 meters or so you will see a large machine. It sells parking permits in increments of 10 to 20 minutes. Get out the magic coin purse. Pay for the time you want. Put the ticket on your dashboard. Lock the car. Come back on time.

If you are careful, you might get a bonus from one of these machines. Parking is free over the "noon hour" which might last for as long as two hours. If, however, you arrive during that free time and want to park until some time after it is over, your only options are to pay for the remainder of the free time, or to come back just as it ends. Sometimes an irritation.

Crisis in Sarlat

Jacques was driving as we entered Sarlat in southwestern France. Now you would think that a Frenchman who had been a jet pilot could easily drive in France, wouldn't you? Doesn't seem to work that way. He handed me a Michelin guide and pointed to a spot on a small-print map of the city, saying: "Find me that parking area." Five minutes later, I still had not located our ever changing position on the map. He grabbed the book back and said: "The navigator is dismissed."

He quickly turned left, and left again, and found himself blocked in a narrow street behind a large truck that was being unloaded. The workers glanced at us and continued to unload. Jack was following in another car, and a third unfortunate turned into the dead end behind Jack. This latter nut began to lean on the horn and made no attempt to back up.

I got out, went to a sidewalk cafe, and moved tables and chairs out of the way. Three cars sped through the opening. After I replaced the furniture, I found the three cars in a pedestrian area, sitting between a group of street musicians and their audience. Our escape route then took us across the square, up a street with a sign saying 18% grade, to the right at the top, down a one-way street against traffic, to a – thank God – parking lot. As we stopped, I said to Jacques: "The driver is fired." We later shared a beer at a table in that square, hoping that nobody recognized us.

Police

Police are generally friendly, courteous and helpful. They are the best ones from whom to ask directions. If you have an accident, they will go to great lengths to be of assistance. Now don't worry about accidents. I have never had one (knock on my wooden head) in Europe. Once while walking in the heart of Paris I stopped a traffic policeman to ask for directions. He immediately whipped out a large, well worn book with detailed maps of Paris. Something tells me I wasn't the first person to ask him for directions. If you are standing on the sidewalk, studying a map, you might be approached by a person who offers to assist you. Again, most people are nice if you give them a chance. Besides, most educated people in Europe are multilingual. Many people are just itching to practice their English skills.

Be careful how you address the police in France if you don't want to offend. The famous gendarme is a country policeman, like a sheriff's deputy. He is actually a member of the military. This is true in some other European countries. Oh yes, if you need help, the French city policeman doesn't like to be called "gendarme." He is "Monsieur l'agent."

Chapter 7
Public Transportation

Public transportation

Public transportation in Europe is generally excellent, and frequent. Because of the limited availability of parking, most people travel by public means – bus, trolley, subway, or inter-urban train. I have always had a fear of public transportation. If I get on the wrong bus, even in Chicago, I might wind up miles and hours away from where I want to be – with the possibility of once more catching the wrong bus on the way back. That is my idiosyncracy. It need not be yours. The buses and trolleys are numbered. The stops have large signs that show the schedules and routes for each number. The free map of the city that you got from the travel office or the hotel concierge also shows the routes.

Trains

You will have great difficulty relating to European trains. They run on time! They are extremely reliable. Most of them are powered by electricity, so they are very clean.

If you decide to do your own thing in Europe by rail rather than by car, you will have made a choice that is quite popular. Talk to your travel agent about Eurorail tickets. You can travel all over: unlimited miles, crossing most any border. The only limit is the number of days for which your ticket is valid. It is one of the best and most economical ways to have an self-conducted tour of Europe.

Sounds nice. Why don't we do it ourselves? There are several reasons. First and foremost, by rail you tend to see the larger cities and not the little country villages. We love the cities, but we love the little villages more. We would feel constrained by a Eurorail pass. Does that mean that I don't recommend it. No way. We each have different tastes and different interests. Depending on your tastes and interests, you can go it alone by car, go it alone by rail, mix the two, join a tour, or stay home. Each option is the right choice for somebody and the wrong choice for somebody else.

If you travel by rail, I'd recommend a second class compartment. If you don't know what a compartment is, you should watch the movie *Murder on the Orient Express.* It gives you graphic images of the layout of European railway carriages. They are quite comfortable. If any part of your agenda is firm, or if you are planning to buy a Eurorail ticket, I'd recommend that you make the purchase before leaving home. Any good travel agency will help you. Or you can make your own reservation by Internet. And if you want a non-smoking compartment, make sure that is arranged in advance too.

I once took a second class train from Newcastle, England to Glasgow, Scotland with a transfer in Edinburgh. The trains were on time and clean. The seats were quite comfortable.

Another time I took an overnight train from Paris to Madrid. There were four seats and four men in a single second class compartment. This was a totally different experience. The seats were quite uncomfortable, since they were collapsible to make room for the bunk beds that folded down from the wall. Nobody spoke, except for one old man who exchanged three phrases with me in the course of the trip. I think the reason is that there is no place to escape to if you become too well acquainted with your compartment mates and find any of them offensive. However, it is not a bad way to travel, being economical and somewhat restful. One nice thing about this mode of travel is that there is no hassle in the middle of the night for a passport check. It was all done for us while we slept.

France has a relatively new, very high speed train called the TGV. That means "train grande vitesse" or very fast train. Imaginative name, what? We have never traveled on the TGV, but one of our sons did when he and his wife came to visit our rented farmhouse in Provence. They loved it.

Nancy and I have traveled on the Japanese equivalent of the TGV, and were properly impressed. Smooth as glass. Fast as lightning. Able to leap tall buildings. On our Japanese ride, the train was full, so we had to stand in the aisle for the three hour trip between Kyoto and Tokyo. It was an overnight sleeper car ride when I was on my way home from army service forty years earlier. What progress!

There is a good reason why we have never traveled by TGV. You must have a seat reservation. We always considered the possibility that the plane might be late, or that we might, God willing, get a bump. For those reasons we have stuck with the rented car. To each his own.

The Vienna express

Ed and April were living in Brussels. They found that they didn't need a car. For extended travel they took trains. They especially liked night trains, because it gave them an inexpensive room for the night. They were on limited means, so they slept sitting up. Even a couchette, however, is still less expensive than a hotel.

On one trip Ed and his daughter left Paris at 11:30 p.m. when the city was just waking up. They arrived in Karlsruhe at 6:00 a.m. after a short night's sleep. Then they caught a local train to Bingen, Germany where they boarded the Rhine steamer at 8:30 a.m. Dinner in Paris, breakfast on the Rhine. They spent one night in Cologne and took another night train to Copenhagen – another night's sleep. Ed reports that it is quite easy to do if you go a bit off-season.

Trolleys and buses

I don't have the same fear of trolleys and subways that I have of buses. That is probably because they are constrained to run on tracks. The conventions are the same as for buses. Study the route map at the trolley or bus stop, and pick the route number that takes you where you want to go. If you can't figure it out, ask one of the other patrons to help you. People are quite helpful in these circumstances. You don't need much language skill. Pointing and pronouncing the name of your desired destination will go a long way toward establishing communication.

Buy your ticket before boarding the vehicle. There will be a ticket vending machine at the stop or in a nearby newspaper, magazine and tobacco kiosk. The tickets are on an honor system, and there is nobody on the vehicle to sell you a ticket or to punch it. On the trolley or bus there will be a machine near the door. You are expected to insert your ticket to have it stamped. Just watch what your fellow passengers do. Occasionally an inspector comes on board to see if anyone is cheating. Don't.

I didn't understand the honor system the first time I was in Vienna. I went everywhere on the trolley, waiting for a conductor to sell me a ticket. I kept wondering where he was hiding. Fortunately none of the inspectors ever came by before I learned the system.

If you need to transfer on surface transportation, you have to ask for a transfer ticket. I have never done that, so I leave it to your own ingenuity.

Two examples of public transportation stand out as worth your serious consideration. The trolley cars in Vienna have picture windows. This is great in a city that was the capital of an empire, and is full of beautiful buildings and monuments. The other is the red double decker bus in London. It is truly famous. Besides, if you climb the circular stair to the top level, you get a marvelous view of another city that was the capital of an empire, and is full of beautiful buildings and monuments. Speaking of that, tickets are sold on the buses in the U.K., but you would be prudent to have the correct change in hand – 70 pence.

Subways

You buy your ticket at the bottom of the stairway or escalator that leads into the subway. You can buy it from a ticket agent or from a vending machine. The tickets are all the same price, no matter how long or short a distance you are going. The vending machines are electronic and probably speak more languages than the ticket agent does. Of course, if your coin purse is short of funds, you will need to deal with the agent. If you plan to take the subway a number of times you would be well advised to buy a book of tickets. It is quite an economy. In

London one can obtain a pass that is good for all public transportation as well as the subway. You need to have passport photos, and you must pay to have the pass made. But, since it is good for years, the savings can be considerable.

The subway routes are extremely well documented on large signs at the entrances and on the platforms. Just pick the route that goes where you want to go, look at the name of the stop at the end of the route – the end that is on the far side of your selected stop. Then go to the correct side of the track, which is also well marked. If you need to transfer, just leave your subway car and follow the signs to the next route. It might be on the same track, or it might be a good walk and several escalators away. These directions are also well marked. A machine will eat your ticket as you leave the station.

Beware of overconfidence

Jack and June had joined us for their first trip to France. We ended our trip with a few days in Paris. The first morning Jack and I decided to return the car to the airport, since we didn't need it any more. Nancy said that she would take June to Notre Dame by subway and wait for us there.

Sure enough, she found the local subway station with no problem. She bought tickets with no problem. She found Notre Dame on the big map at the subway, and from it found the correct subway line, going in the proper direction. All went well until they left the subway and came up into the sunlight. Where were they? Nothing looked familiar. That was when Nancy realized that "Notre Dame' is a common name for a number of churches. It took a second subway ride to correct the error. This is another reason to buy books of tickets.

Taxis

Taxis are almost invariably cleaner, and taxi drivers are almost invariably better dressed and better mannered than in the U.S. Perhaps the difference is one of culture. Perhaps it is a result of the volume of public transportation. At any rate, a taxi ride is usually efficient, safe and comfortable. If you go to London, I'd advise you to take a taxi when convenient. The taxi drivers there must pass a rigorous test before being licensed. The course of study lasts three to four years.

They know every street and alley. They know where roads are blocked by construction. And best of all, they know all of the places that might interest a tourist. They are among the best and least expensive tourist guides in the world.

The taxi fares are modest, and the drivers are honest in most of Western Europe. Even so, it is always best to verify the expected cost of your ride before you enter the taxi. You might not be aware of the distance between where you are and where you want to be.

Certainly verify the fare in Greece, and make sure that the meter is turned back. The rates are extremely low. For this reason some cabbies have developed a habit of "forgetting" to reset the meter. This way the unsuspecting passenger pays for his ride and also for that of one or more other customers who rode before him. Even if you get caught in this scam, the fare is still very low.

Like in the U.S., the cabbies rely on tips for a significant part of their income. Tip about 15% of the fare. Don't be an "ugly American."

Why a Japanese story?

This story doesn't really belong in a book about European travel, but Nancy insisted that I add it. I have to admit that it brings back entertaining memories.

Our daughter who had worked a year in London also had worked a year in Tokyo. Again, as good parents, we went to visit. Besides, we had lived in Kyoto for a time while I was in the army. It would be nice to see how things had changed.

We went by train from Tokyo to Kyoto to reminisce. Susie had rented a room in a Japanese inn for us. We arrived at the train station late in the evening and joined one of two lines of people waiting for taxis. The taxis came fast, and the lines shortened half as fast. When we reached the head of our line, the taxis would swerve by us and go to the other line. The cabbies consider "gaijin" or foreigners, to be a bother. Finally one sleepy cabby failed to notice our round eyes. Susie gave him a card with the hotel address. He sucked in his breath through his teeth with a hiss, meaning that he was frustrated. He also became lost and hissed a lot more. Susie had adequate Japanese fluency to get him to the hotel, but at one point she turned to us and said, "I hope he gets there before he hyperventilates."

Boats

In places there are long stretches of river between bridges. For this reason, you will sometimes find it convenient to cross a river on a ferry. They are inexpensive, and cross the river repeatedly without any "rest stop" between trips. You won't have to wait long. If you explore the castles along the Rhine in the area of the Lorelei, you will find the ferries to be indispensable.

There are also tour boats on pretty rivers and lakes, such as the Rhine and the Bodensee or Lake Constance. You will find that their schedule is not quite as reliable. You won't be able to take your car on the tour boat with you. Plan a return to your starting point by train if time is a problem for you.

Chapter 8
Lodging

Availability

There is a wide variety of lodging options in Europe. You can find just about anything you might wish. There are the usual multi-storied hotels with all the amenities, many of them operated by large U.S. hotel chains. There are also chains of economy hotels in a variety of price ranges. There are mom and pop hotels of two to five storeys with as few as three or four rooms or as many as thirty or forty. There are innumerable bed and breakfast facilities. There are many inns and hostels, some with just a few rooms on the storey above the corner bar. You can stay in a 400-year-old chateau or a 900-year-old castle. You can even spend the night in a cave. And you can rent a house or an apartment by the week or month.

We rarely make advance reservations for lodging. We will do so if we plan to stay at a special place, or if we feel that facilities might be crowded due to a holiday. We will do so if we plan to stay in a large city at the beginning of our trip and don't want to rent a car until we leave that city. We will also do so if we expect to arrive late in the day when most of the available rooms have been taken. This is one of the advantages of traveling just before or just after the main tourist season.

You can go where you want, when you want, and still not be overly concerned about finding good lodging at a reasonable price.

You can gain a lot of information about the types and availability of lodging through guide books, through Internet, and through literature obtained from embassies or consulates. Study them, not so much to select your lodging for each night, but to gain a familiarity with the options. However, if a few specific facilities appeal to you, you might want to write to them for reservations.

There are two places where we have stayed several times, and have made reservations to ensure that rooms are set aside for us – not to guarantee a place to sleep, but to guarantee the treat that we know we have in store. One is a castle, and the other is the farmhouse of a chateau. You won't find a separate topic in this chapter for castles and chateaux. They are hard to classify. Each building has unique features. Most are very expensive. Some are available at surprisingly low cost. The best that I can do to help you is to illustrate by example.

A thousand years old

In a piece of literature from the French tourist office I found information about castles and chateaux that offered nightly lodging. Most were quite expensive. One, in the broader Loire Valley, was most reasonably priced. I made a reservation by mail.

It turned out that the small castle was almost a thousand years old. The room was comfortable. The host and the housekeeper were most friendly, and were generous with stories about local lore, including a tale that an infant son of Richard the Lionheart was interred in the ruined chapel that was part of the castle. We went to and from our large room, with fireplace, via a real turret. On the mantle of the fireplace was a medieval sculpture of St. Peter.

The castle was a wonderful, convenient location from which to explore other chateaux of the Loire Valley. We returned a few years later for another visit. This time we were given a room in another turret. Imagine waking up in the morning to see a circular ceiling. It was a distinctive reminder of where we were and of the history of the building.

Mont St. Michel

We finally managed to include Mont St. Michel in the itinerary of one of our trips to France. It is worth a trip all by itself. As we approached the area we passed a new sign advertising a bed and breakfast. Since it was about the time to find lodging for the night, I turned off the main highway onto the indicated country lane. We found a farmhouse surrounded by a walled courtyard. It had been the home of the manager of an estate whose chateau was destroyed in WWII. The casing of an unexploded bomb was still lying in the woods behind the farmhouse.

The place was beautiful. The hosts were most gracious. We stayed two nights, and wished we could stay longer. Our host placed an American flag on our breakfast table. When I told him I was doing research on my ancestors from Luxembourg, he said that he had no Luxembourg flag. That day I bought one in the village and gave it to him. When we returned several years later, the Luxembourg flag had joined the American one on our table.

We were treated as guests, not customers. In the evening the host offered us a glass of home-made Calvados from the cellar. The children were invited to meet us, and we played silly table games with the grandchildren in front of a roaring fireplace. Of course we hope to return again. This is a place where we will make a reservation and commit to a date – for good reason.

Selecting a place for the night

There are a number of published ratings of hotels for each country. You can find them in a bookshop either here or in your target country. The most reliable rating system is that of Michelin. I seem to refer to that company a lot. Really, they are the standard of the industry.

I have a five-year-old copy of the Michelin guide to French hotels and restaurants. French natives who travel or eat out frequently would never be caught without the latest copy. Personally, I find that the book ages well, and that the quoted prices change only gradually.

The Michelin guide gives hotels a rating on a scale of one to five stars. The one star hotels are almost invariably very basic, with bath and toilet down the hall. The three star hotels tend to be places where you don't just spend the night, but enjoy the amenities. They can be quite pricey. The two star hotels usually have comfortable rooms with bathing facilities. We stay almost exclusively at two star hotels, and have rarely been disappointed.

Look at the sign above the front door of a hotel. It shows the star rating of the facility. If the hotel is in the Michelin book, you can be guaranteed that it will be acceptable. If it is not in the book, it needs closer inspection. In Germany, Austria and Luxembourg the star rating above the door is generally a reliable indication, just as in the Michelin guide. In France, the home of Michelin, there are a number of hotels that are rated by other agencies. We have found their quality to be far less reliable. So what do you do then? Ask to look at a room. The proprietor will not be offended. You will probably be shown a number of rooms. If you like a room that you are shown, and if you like the price, ask for that specific room.

The local ratings in Spain, Portugal and Italy are different. You might be disappointed in a hotel that they rate as two star. The three star hotels are more similar to the two star hotels elsewhere. Even so, these three star hotels are 20 to 40% less expensive than two star hotels in other countries.

Nude bather

Customs are different in Europe in a number of ways. I was in Friedrichshafen with our older daughter on my only tour. Mary Beth was traveling with a college choir. The night in Friedrichshafen was spent in a three star hotel with a swimming pool. After dinner the young people migrated to the pool. I sat in a deck chair and watched the antics.

Suddenly a man came out of the locker room, stark naked, and strolled around the pool to another deck chair. He carefully covered his head – only his head – with the towel. The next morning I conducted a survey of the choir. Nobody could remember the color of the man's eyes. Testimony to the effectiveness of a well-placed towel.

Reservations

If you find a place that especially attracts you while you are studying travel literature, and if you are prepared to commit yourself to be in a specific place on a specific day, then write for a reservation.

The proprietor will either be able to understand English, or has a friend who will translate for him. Seldom have I been asked for a deposit. In such a case I have sent a check. When I arrived at the lodging and paid for the room, the original, uncashed check was returned to me. Don't wait until the last minute to ask for a reservation. The response to international mail can take two or three weeks. If you have any doubt about where the hotel is, ask to have directions mailed to you. I well remember looking for a hotel in Rouen, France where we had made advance reservations. We drove in circles for an hour before we found that the hotel was in a pedestrian area and could not be reached by car. Note that to reserve a room in Rome, the price must be paid in advance to reserve it, and there is no refund in the advent of a cancellation.

Bargain basement

The least expensive lodging can most easily be found through the tourist office that is usually found in or near any train station. Many of the inexpensive hotels are located in the general neighborhood of the station. Be sure to ask if they are clean and safe. Train stations are not always located in the best part of town.

There are a number of economy hotel chains in Europe that you won't find in travel guides. Your best way of finding them is by spotting them at the exits of expressways. Stop off and ask to be shown a room. These chains are similar to the economy chains in the U.S. They are frequented by business people, like salesmen, who travel. Unlike their U.S. counterparts the rooms are smaller and are sparkling clean. The decor is usually a bit garish, but after all, you are only spending the night.

In one of the chains the toilet and shower facilities are not in the rooms, but are located near the elevator on each floor. After use, the shutting of the door triggers an automatic spray that washes and disinfects the room. So, when you go to use the toilet, rest assured that any standing water is from the cleaning system, and not from the previous user.

These economy chains are usually closed from about 10 a.m. until 5 p.m. Part of the economy. But, if you stop when the manager is at his or her desk, you will find a most gracious welcome. Don't be surprised if the manager speaks English. If you find a chain that attracts you, then pick up a catalog that lists all of the chain's facilities in that country. The catalog will list locations and prices. You can reserve rooms by phone. You can also cancel rooms by phone. This makes your travel very flexible. Some chains have a computer terminal by the door so that you can make your reservation even if nobody is manning the desk. In some, the terminal will access any hotel in the chain.

Since hotel rooms in larger cities tend to be significantly more expensive than in villages, we often reserve an economy room by phone a day or two before arriving in the big city. Then, if we see a hotel or a bed and breakfast that attracts us, we cancel the economy reservation. The chain never seems to have a problem with this practice, since they are usually fully booked by evening.

When in Paris we always stay at the Etap hotel near the Porte d'Orleans on the south side of the city. The hotel is only half a kilometer away from the métro, the subway. It is clean and well furnished. A room costs about $50. Beat that for a large city.

Timing

If you want to be flexible and do most of your traveling without advance reservations, then you would do well to decide by about 5 p.m. where you will spend the night. This avoids the need to look for a room at the last minute. All of us have experienced the frustrating problem of looking for a room in an area where everything has been booked because of some local celebration that we didn't know about. The idea of sleeping in the car is never attractive.

If you decide to stay in an economy chain hotel, you must either make a telephone reservation or you must visit the hotel before 10 a.m. or after 5 p.m. The desk clerk will give you a security code so that you can gain access to the hotel and your room at any hour of the day or night. This is far better service than that of a few small hotels that close their doors during the middle of the day, even to registered guests.

If you are staying in a mom and pop hotel, you will find that they lock the doors about 10 p.m. If you plan to have a late evening at a restaurant, or at a concert or movie, or at a casino, then make sure that the manager of the hotel shows you how to gain entry "after hours." Normally the manager will inform you without being asked. Sometimes the key to your room is on a ring with the key to the outside door. Sometimes you will be given a series of numbers to open the door by means of a digital pad.

Which tower is which?

Jerry had checked into his hotel in Prague. He decided to go for a walk to see the sights. Knowing that he has a tendency to get lost, he looked for a landmark. Finally he spotted a tall tower. He felt that as long as he could see the tower, he could locate his hotel. As he walked, he would occasionally seek an open space from which he could spot the tower. It was only after he had walked a long distance that he realized he was lost again. It turned out that the wall of the old city had many towers, all of which looked alike.

Mom and pop hotels

The most common hotels, and the ones we use most often, are small ones of ten to forty rooms. These tend to be comfortable buildings up to 300 years old. They have character. They also have managers and customers who are inclined to visit with foreigners. If you travel in a foreign country, you might as well learn something about the people of that country. This is one of the greatest benefits of this sort of travel. You can learn more about the character of a country from one night in a mom and pop hotel than you can from any canned lecture by a tourist guide.

These small hotels usually have rooms in a variety of price ranges, with toilet and bath or shower, with bath or shower, or with all facilities down the hall. All are fine. Even the "down the hall" facilities are clean and sanitary. You pay your money and you take your choice. If you haven't looked at the room in advance, you pay your money and you take your chances.

If your mom and pop hotel has a restaurant, you will want to have dinner there unless you have a strong reason to do otherwise. The room is reasonably priced because of the expectation of income from the restaurant. You will be treated more as a guest of the house than as someone who just stopped in off the street. If you stay for more than one night and have wine with your meal, the waiter will store the remainder of your bottle and bring it back to your table at your next dinner.

In a European hotel, particularly a small one, you are really treated as a guest. To illustrate. I once spent four days in a small hotel in Larochette, Luxembourg. The proprietors sat and visited with me in the lounge on several occasions. They offered me a drink or two that never found their way onto my bill. They told me of interesting places to visit. They provided a special menu one evening at my request, and they gave me the last night of lodging free. Finally, they asked me to email them on my return home so that they would know that I had arrived safely.

The phantom bellhop

We were on our way north after a week in Provence. The route we had selected took us through the city of Sisteron in the middle of nowhere, with a huge old fortress overlooking a beautiful river valley. We found a charming little hotel and prepared to settle in for the night. The bellhop suggested that I park the car in the garage, which was located down a steep grade beneath the building. I did so with no problem. He then took our bags and showed us to a tiny elevator that barely held the four of us. When we arrived two floors up, there he was, waiting for us and not breathing hard. We saw him do this several times that evening. He is either in excellent shape, or he is twins.

The next morning I tried to get the car out of the garage. It involved backing up from the space, straight up the ramp. I never quite made it, since the ramp had more slope than the car had power. The bellhop took over. He revved the engine, held the brake, and then let go. He made it, gave us a satisfied smile, and disappeared. Jack rather appropriately named him the phantom bellhop.

Bed and breakfast

If you are traveling through the countryside of Ireland or Great Britain, the bed and breakfast is always a good choice. The same is generally true on the European continent. In our own country a bed and breakfast tends to be an expensive night where you are impressed by the antiques and by the decor. In Europe, the normal furnishings of a bed and breakfast are also antique. This is not interior decoration. It is merely a fact of life. Furnishings were well made and were expected to last for a long time – several lifetimes.

You can expect to find the cost of a night's lodging to be generally less than that at a mom and pop hotel, unless the bed and breakfast has some special attraction, such as an age over 300 years. Different world! You can expect clean facilities and a private entrance. You can expect a host who is knowledgeable about the local history and attractions. You can also expect a delicious breakfast to be included in the price of the room, available at an hour of your choosing. Breakfast is the time for you to quiz your host about local history and tourist sites. But remember, he or she is as curious about your country as you are about the one you are visiting. Fair is fair.

House rental

If you know that you want to stay in a specific area for a number of days, then you should consider renting a house. Usually you will do this in advance. The reservation invariably requires a down payment, and usually full payment shortly before you arrive. A personal check is not acceptable. You need to obtain a bank draft in the currency of the country. In southern France there are many charming old houses that have been purchased and remodeled by Englishmen as off-season getaways. The owners help reduce their expenses by renting the house during times when they know they won't be there. We have rented a farmhouse in Provence and one in Dordogne. Delightful! And economical!

It is worth noting here one special region with many vacation houses that can be rented by the week. This is in Bavaria in the area of Garmish-Partenkirchen. The terrain is mountainous, with many historic and natural attractions. The local custom is to paint scenes on the stuccoed facade of the houses. If you get tired of touring the countryside, you can just sit in the front yard and admire the view of your house. Besides, the area is noted for its hand-carved wooden figures. It is almost impossible to return home without having purchased several carvings.

Hotel conventions

The conventions for use of a hotel in Europe are a bit different. When you check in they don't normally ask for the license number of your car. It is either in a rental lot under different management or it is on the street near the hotel. The management couldn't care less about it. You probably will not be asked for a credit card. Credit cards are not popular yet in Germany, and most of Europe is on the honor system. They trust that you will pay when you leave.

You will be asked how many nights you plan to stay. Our usual answer is that we will decide tomorrow if we will stay longer, depending upon what we learn as we explore the surroundings (and unsaid, how we enjoy the hotel.) Note that if you stay for more than one night, the room rate might decline.

A number of years ago the desk clerk at a hotel would ask to see your passport, and then put it in the hotel safe. He also asked that you fill out a registration card with a lot of personal data. The police would stop by each night and pick up the cards, for public security. If you have never seen it, you might rent the original film of *The Jackal* to learn what the conventions were, and the security that they were intended to provide. Today the hotel asks for minimal information unless you want to exchange currency. As you will see in Chapter 15, a hotel is not a place where you want to do that.

In Spain and Portugal the hotel clerk will probably ask for your passport. He is only using it to note your passport number in case you skip out without paying. Not quite so trusting as people in the more northerly part of Europe. He will return the passport to you the next time you pass by the reception desk.

In most hotels your room key will be on a ring with a large chunk of metal. This is a signal to deposit your key at the desk when you leave the building. You ask for it by room number when you return, or you pick it off a hook, depending on the size of the hotel and the sophistication of the hosts.

Floor numbering is different from that in the U.S. and can be confusing. The ground floor is known as the ground floor and not as the first floor. If there are rooms on the ground floor, they will be numbered as 15, 22, etc. What we know as the second floor is the first floor in Europe – the first floor above the ground. Room numbers will be 115, 122, etc. If the key doesn't open the door to your room easily, check to see if you are on the correct floor.

One more word of advice from Jerry, who seems to get lost more often than most. Always ask the hotel for a business card. If you get lost in your meanderings, the card will always get you home. Don't rely on the name of your hotel to guide a cabby. In a large city many hotels can have the same name. Besides, if you ever return to the area, the card will guide you back to a hotel that you liked.

Modern hotels, the more expensive kind, tend to have all of the amenities. The older and smaller the hotel, the less the amenities. Your room in a small old hotel might not have a television set. However, if it does have one, the channels will usually include one or two in English.

Breakfast is served as a part of the price of the room in many countries in continental Europe. By definition it is always included at a bed and breakfast. In recent years French, Spanish and Portuguese hotels have stopped providing it as a part of the room. In Luxembourg, Germany, Austria and the British Isles the breakfast is not only free, but extremely generous. It will usually include a soft boiled egg, various cold cuts and cheeses, and lots of bread and jam. Did I mention cold cereals? If you are comparing prices between standard hotels and a bed and breakfast, add $5 to $8 to the advertised price of the hotel. That is, unless you aren't inclined to eat breakfast.

Breakfast at a hotel is usually served between 8 and 10 a.m. In a bed and breakfast you will be asked to state a time that you want your breakfast. The host usually has to heat some of the food, and prefers that you be served while it is hot. It might include a quiche or poached eggs. If you name too early a time, your request will be honored, but eyebrows will be raised.

The people who clean up and make beds are generally poorly paid. Many are immigrants who are supporting poor relatives at home – Turks in Germany, Portuguese in Luxembourg, Algerians in France. Leave a tip. It need not be a large amount. The equivalent of a dollar is sufficient.

Finally, it is well to be aware of the distinct possibility that at some time or other you will find yourself in a poor quality hotel. This will probably be because you didn't do your homework properly, such as arriving late or failing to ask to see a room. Go with the flow. Keep your sense of humor. If you give in to a moment's frustration, you can ruin a wonderful trip.

Is it all wonderful? No. I too have a problem, and I might as well grumble a bit here. We usually travel with Jack and June. They are wonderful companions, but have no language facility other than English. Nancy is competent in French, but defers to me when there is something significant to negotiate. I have "street smarts" in a few languages. So, I am always the one who must find the night's lodging. It so happens that we generally manage to find satisfactory lodging at a lower price than we might have expected. Each evening my three companions expect that I will find lodging at least as good as the best we have experienced to date, and at less expense. By the end of a three week trip the pressure becomes rather significant.

There was, however one exception. We were in Spain, approaching Santiago de Compostela on the expressway from the south. Not being in the mood to drive in a large city, looking for a hotel, we left the expressway near a small town that we could see in a valley. I asked the toll clerk if there were any hotels there. She said no. I didn't believe her, because I could see a few factory buildings. The town was Caldas de Reyes. There were three hotels. The first one that we tried was new and beautiful, with generous rooms, a comfortable lounge, and a large outside balcony. The price was the equivalent of $25 a night. Nobody ever asked me to improve on that deal.

Which floor is which?

We were on one of our occasional visits to Luxembourg, the home of my ancestors. Since Luxembourg is small and seems to restrict the hotel chains, the price of hotel rooms tends to be higher than in neighboring countries. For this reason we spent the night at an Etap hotel, part of an inexpensive French hotel chain, in Thionville, just south of the border.

The ladies left us as soon as we obtained the keys to our rooms. It had something to do with the amount of liquid they had drunk since our last stop. Jack and I finished arrangements at the hotel desk and headed for the elevator. Our rooms were numbers 212 and 213. As the elevator approached the floor, we heard familiar voices laughing. When the door to the elevator opened, we found our wives in hysterics. They had gone to the second floor instead of the third (European floor numbering systems.) They were laughing at themselves and were hoping that we wouldn't catch them in their error. Needless to say, they were delighted to find us in the same error. We tried to say that we did it just to make them feel better, but it didn't fly.

Chapter 9
Food

The ultimate go-no go gauge

If you have read this far into the book, you are probably serious about trying to do your own thing in Europe. Here is your ultimate point of decision.. Should you do it or not? It really depends upon your attitude toward food. If you enjoy trying new things, go for it. If you are somewhat willing to try new things providing they aren't too different, then you can have an enjoyable trip, but will miss some of the adventure. You should also take along some snacks to carry you through times when you are hungry but don't find anything that appeals to you. If you only like steak and potatoes, then stay home. You would be frustrated, and hungry, in Europe.

Hamburger?

I was in Grenoble in the French Alps on my first trip abroad. This one was paid for by my employer, and I was working. After a few days of French food, I felt like having something American for a change. I ordered a hamburger. It was a hamburger all right, a patty of fried ground beef on a plate, topped with a fried egg. This is where I first discovered that the name doesn't necessarily tell you what the dish is. I learned later that if the menu had said "Hamburger Americain" it would have been a patty of raw ground beef.

Breakfast

Breakfast is your easiest meal, unless you want bacon, eggs and cornflakes. If you do, it will cost you dearly. Europeans just don't breakfast like Americans. In Russia, breakfast will include a hot cereal like cream of wheat, cole slaw, cold peas, hard boiled eggs, and tea. In England the full English breakfast – excellent, by the way – consists of poached or fried eggs, bacon that is a cut which includes both American and Canadian style bacon, broiled tomatoes, sauteed mushrooms, a rather bland fried sausage called a banger, and of course, toast and orange marmalade. In Germany, Austria and Luxembourg breakfast includes a soft boiled egg, hard rolls, cheeses, cold cuts, cold cereal, yogurt and fruit. In France breakfast consists of croissants, crusty bread and jams. Yes, you can get cold cereal, but the milk will probably taste quite different to you. Not bad. Different.

So what are your choices? First of all, you can do without breakfast. Second, you can take the breakfast that is offered – if it is offered – by the hotel where you are staying. A few years ago breakfast came with the price of the room. It still does in Germany, Austria, Luxembourg and the British Isles. It does not in France, Spain or Portugal, except in bed and breakfast facilities. I haven't had the opportunity for a few years to review the breakfast conventions in other countries. You would be well advised to ask if it is included when you register for your room. If breakfast is not offered, it is probably available for a price. Our experience has been that is not a good buy except in the economy hotel chains.

Your third choice is to look for breakfast somewhere other than where you spent the night. We have often stopped at a sidewalk cafe for a cup of coffee. Then we drop into a bakery and buy some pastries, a croissant, a loaf of local bread, or just a baguette, the long slender loaf that is the standard French bread. It is delicious. In a highly scientific and detailed survey we have determined that at least fifty percent of the baguettes being carried on the street have had a bite taken out of them. I challenge you to resist. If you search diligently, you can find a bakery that has small tables and serves coffee. The coffee will be brewed on the spot, like an espresso.

As long as we are talking about coffee, there are three kinds that are generally available, other than Italian cappuccino, which is ambrosia. One is espresso. You might be served espresso if you simply ask for coffee. The second is a large cup of coffee, the kind you are accustomed to at home. To get it, ask for a *large* cup. It is at least twice as strong as American coffee. Many a European has told me that he doesn't like American coffee where you can see the bottom of the cup. I have come to agree with them. The third type of coffee is the large cup with up to 50% hot milk. If you don't think you can handle strong coffee, go for this one. If you want to try the espresso, plan on adding some sugar or a twist of lemon peel if it is available. It cuts any tendency toward bitterness.

Lunch

Our favorite lunch is a picnic. We go to a grocery store and buy a loaf of local bread, local cheese, local wine and some fruit. Then we go to a park, or to a rest stop if we are on the expressway. It is a wonderful, relaxing experience. And it is a real bargain. Note the local products that I recommended above. They tend to blend very well together. The bread doesn't vary much, but over the centuries European communities have become artists at matching the flavors of their cheese and wine. Try other breads, particularly the darker ones that are sometimes called country bread or peasant bread. All of these products are significantly less expensive than at home. The bread and cheese are about half our normal price. You can get a bottle of quite acceptable wine for the equivalent of $2 to $3. We have occasionally found tolerable wine on sale in a supermarket for as little as $1 a bottle. While traveling in Germany where most of the wines are white, we were delighted to learn that white wines don't need to be chilled to be enjoyable.

Parks usually have picnic tables, or at least benches, most often along streams where it is nice to relax and watch the scenery as you eat. In most countries, with Spain as the exception, there are usually picnic areas along the roads, especially at rest stops on expressways.

A word of help for your shopping. Most supermarkets operate in much the same manner that you are accustomed to. The bread will probably be sold at a bakery counter near the entrance to the store. You pay for it there. The produce department has a scale with pictures of the various fruits and vegetables. Put your fruit on the scale in a plastic bag from a dispenser. If you select apples, locate the picture that corresponds to your apples, and press the picture to trigger a button. The scale will print a sticker with the appropriate price for the weight it senses. Put the sticker on the bag.

Oh yes, remember that on the continent the weights are in kilograms, not pounds. A kilogram is the equivalent of 2.2 pounds. If the price on a product says 5 francs, then it means 5 francs per kilogram or just over 2 francs per pound. If you forget, you will only do so once. If the clerk cuts you a kilo of cheese, you will have to decide what to do with the portion you can't manage to eat. We found that 300 to 400 grams of cheese is just about right for the four of us. Don't ask for half a kilogram. You probably won't be understood, even if you speak the local language. Ask for 500 grams.

Another choice for lunch is to go to a restaurant. We have found this to be time-consuming and rather expensive. If we aren't picnicking, we would rather stop at a sidewalk cafe for something simple and fast. If you do so, pick one away from the streets with expensive shops. The cafes mimic the price structures of the stores in the area.

After finding it difficult to adjust to the late (9:00 or later) dinner hour in Spain, we found it better to eat a restaurant meal in the middle of the day and then to snack or picnic in the evening. Eventually we learned that the Spanish also eat their heavy meal at noon. No wonder they like the siesta. They need it.

A delightful option is to grab a sandwich and a beer or wine at a local corner stand. In Vienna there is an inimitable hot sausage called the kreuzerkrainer, a sort of Polish sausage with chunks of cheese imbedded in it. In France the cold ham sandwiches on a section of baguette are light and refreshing. A French specialty is a "croque monsieur," a hot ham sandwich covered with melted cheese. In London we once had a sandwich that consisted of a few pieces of crab meat placed between two thin slices of plain white bread. It looked totally blah. It tasted marvelous. Hundreds of people take daily lunch in the central square in Luxembourg City. It has everything from a beer and sausage stand to an expensive restaurant where the waiters are dressed in tuxedos. All of this is done out of doors on the square.

Another option for lunch is to stop in at a pub. All countries have pubs of one sort or another. The drinks will be very good. The food will be excellent about a third of the time, tolerable about a third of the time, and revolting the remaining third of the time. Go ahead, try it. Good luck!

There are a few fast food places, some of them familiar American chains. The food selection is a bit broader than it is here. The hamburgers, fries and shakes (no shakes in Spain) taste virtually identical to the U.S. variety. The prices will be about half again as high as here. Oh yes, they serve beer and wine.

There are also some hole-in-the-wall specialty food outlets. In Paris, if the proprietor of a hole-in-the-wall looks Algerian, you would do well to stay away from the meat selections. But go for the French fries. The Algerians know how to make them better than the French do. I have tried Algerian sausage, thank you. I'll stick to the fries.

Dinner

Dinner is where you should expect your real culinary adventures to happen. Tasty as your options are for breakfast and lunch, the variety of foods is limited compared to dinner menus. If you are fussy about your food, this is also where your adaptability will be challenged. It is handy if you have a "garbage can" in your group. That is someone who can eat and enjoy anything. I am the designated garbage can for our group of four. If anybody gets a nasty surprise when the food is served, it is offered to me in exchange for whatever I have ordered, unless I am already eating something really strange. So, I never know what my meal will be. It is always good. Well, almost always.

Dinner hour in Europe tends to be later in the evening than Americans are accustomed to. Restaurants will be closed and dark until at least 6:30 in the evening, 7:00 in Luxembourg, 7:30 in France, 8:00 in Portugal, 9:00 in Spain. It seems that the farther south you go, the later the dinner hour. It is not uncommon for a Spanish family to begin eating at 11:00 p.m. Not by my digestive system!

Restaurants tend to be small, some with as few as half a dozen tables. Almost all restaurants have the menu posted near the entrance. Restaurant window shopping is an enjoyable sport. Be sure to carry your dictionary, but don't be surprised to learn that it doesn't contain a good number of the terms. Describing dishes with words seems to be as imaginative as preparing them.

Your safest bet, both for price and for compatibility with your taste is to select the menu of the day. Most restaurants have one to three set menus at a fixed price. Such a menu will include at least an appetizer, a main course, and a desert. Sometimes a set menu includes three to six options for each course. The food will be fresh, since it is the specialty of the day. It will be reasonably compatible with your taste buds, since it is aimed at travelers. If you look for the same items on the à la carte menu, you will find that the set menu is a real bargain.

Even the set menu is not a guarantee of the price you will pay, however. In some countries the bread is an extra charge, even though it is delivered as though it were standard with the meal. It is an extra charge, like the coffee with an American breakfast. I well remember an Austrian waiter counting the rolls left in the basket as he added up our bill. In Portugal, not only is the bread an extra, but the waiter will bring to the table several plates of appetizers, called "couverts." These must be paid for separately. If you don't want them, send them back immediately. If you don't reject them promptly, you will pay for them even if you haven't eaten anything.

Your choices of drinks with the meal are virtually unlimited. Of course, each area has a variety of local wines or beers. If that is your taste, and if you don't know what to choose, ask the waiter to recommend something. He will be complimented, and is not likely to bring you the most expensive wine in the house – except in Italy where he might do just that. Ask the price. If water is your drink, don't expect it to be provided without being requested. Although the tap water is quite potable and safe throughout western Europe, people have developed the habit of drinking bottled water. It comes in two varieties, plain water (without gas) and sparkling (gaseous) water. It will come cold, and without ice.

On some set menus a drink is included with your meal. The options are water or the house wine. Coffee is an extra and is ordered separately after you have eaten the meal, including the dessert.

You will not be offered ice unless you request it. Even with alcoholic drinks that are customarily iced, only a small amount of ice will be offered. If you order scotch and water, or pastis, expect that the liquor, the water and the ice will all be brought separately so that you can mix the drink to your taste.

The sequence of dishes in a meal is also different. The salad, if there is one, might be brought after the main course. Bread and cheese will be brought toward the end of the meal, just before the dessert. The cheese will most likely be offered on a tray containing five to twenty five varieties. Take three of four. Interestingly, Europeans tend to butter the bread that they eat with their cheese. If there is a desert it will be the last course, sometimes accompanied by coffee, but usually followed by coffee. After the coffee, you might be urged to order a liqueur, sometimes called a digestive. On some occasions, especially in Italy, it is on the house.

You will not find a small plate for you to use to hold your bread. The custom is for you to place the bread on the tablecloth, to the northwest of your plate. Just before dessert, the waiter will brush all of the crumbs (there will be an abundant supply) off the tablecloth.

Applauding the chef

We were in Les Baux, just south of Avignon in the Rhone delta. Les Baux is a marvelous medieval village on top of a steep cliff, with a ruined castle, a nice little museum, and many shops that sell local crafts and imported junk. It also has a number of little restaurants and hotels. We selected a restaurant built against the side of the cliff. The smooth white walls of the dining room were broken here and there where the naked rock of the cliff projected into the room. It was charming.

The four of us each selected something different from the set menu. All of the dishes were delicious, and all were very well presented. Our host had studied hotel management in Chicago for a year, so the conversation flowed easily. At the end of the meal I asked him if he had been wise enough to marry the chef. He had. We asked him to bring her into the dining room and introduce her. He did. The whole restaurant broke into applause. Yes, we hope to go back there again.

Local specialties

If you want to add to your perspective of regional differences between countries and within a country, try local dishes. The sauerkraut in Alsace-Lorraine is a wonderful compliment to a mixed grill. The seafood on the coasts is done with imagination, especially the salmon in Portugal. The lamb in the United Kingdom and in mountainous areas of the continent is light and tasty. Of course, the continentals don't respect English cooking. They like to say that the English kill their lamb twice – once when they butcher it and once when they cook it. That is funny, but unfair. Veal and pork, particularly breaded pork, are a specialty of Germany. Austria is similar to Germany, but has a love affair with sausages. Try eating mussels in Belgium, fois gras and snails in France. Spices in southern Italy are different from those in northern Italy and the Provence region of France. They are virtually missing in Germany, except in sausages.

You will also find some very unusual dishes if you are so inclined. Sweetbreads, or selected internal organs, are a delicacy in some areas. Snails are a French tradition, but frankly, the French get more enjoyment out of dipping their bread into the garlic sauce than they do from the snails themselves. So do I. Some fish, especially trout and scampi will be served with the heads on to assure you that you are getting what you ordered. "Fruits de mer" or fruit of the sea is a selection of raw shellfish. There is one particular Italian sea snail that stares back at you with a single large red eye. Oh yes, I should have told you to skip this section if you are digestively impaired.

In Spain during the spring the special delicacy is a plate of white unborn eels in a garlic sauce similar to the one the French use for snails. It looks like a plate of spaghetti and tastes like snails, that is if you are courageous enough to try it. In Greece the waiter will take you into the kitchen to select your fish – a large fish. The small fish are deep-fried like smelt, and are served as an appetizer, but with the heads on. The whole fish is eaten.

Remember one thing about these unusual foods. The local people have been eating them for hundreds of years. They like them. They stay healthy. The only problem is our lack of experience with these things, and our lack of tolerance of differences. Remember, if you wanted steak and potatoes you could have stayed home. Speaking of steak and potatoes, France and Switzerland do great things with a thin steak called an entrecôte. It is usually served with a salad and delicious French fries. It makes a great lunch or dinner.

Shrimp eyes

It was a beautiful large restaurant in Arromanche overlooking the Normandy beaches, with rusting caissons providing a sad reminder of the sacrifices that had been made there. Being on the shore of the English Channel, we ordered seafood, a specialty of the house.

Now, Jack is not exactly an adventuresome diner. He does all right if the food has a reasonable resemblance to what he is accustomed to. I had a large platter of "fruits de mer," which was placed in front of me before the others were served – no cooking to delay service. Jack had ordered a plate of boiled scampi. While he waited to be served, he watched with horror as I chewed on the raw seafood.

His plate came. It was a beautiful presentation of two kinds of shrimp. But they all had their heads on, and their little black eyes stared at him with reproach. He managed to eat a few, then a few more as June peeled them for him. But he couldn't manage to finish the plate. He did enjoy the view out the window, though.

Liechtenstein meatloaf

On a trip to Austria and Germany I had twice eaten "leberkäse" or liver cheese for dinner. Leberkäse looks like a thick baloney, and is pan fried. My wife says that I will eat anything. She asked me to not eat it any more that trip out of respect for my cholesterol level. It was easy to concede, since I had eaten my fill of it anyway.

We were spending the night at Lindau, a beautiful town on an island at the eastern end of Lake Constance, the Bodensee. On a last minute inspiration we decided to "collect a country" and drive south for an hour to have dinner in Liechtenstein, the smallest country in Europe. At the restaurant, I had a communication problem with the waitress. My German was weak, and her French and English were nonexistent.

She explained to me that the dish I was asking about was a sort of meatloaf. I ordered it. Guess what I got. Leberkäse!

Tipping

Waiters are better paid in Europe. In some countries they don't have to rely on tips to supplement their wages. For this reason, most of the time (but not quite all of the time) your bill will have a message at the bottom telling you that the tip is included. If the magic words aren't there, as in Spain and Portugal, ask about it. If the tip is not included, you should tip as you would at home. If the tip is included you are not obliged to tip at all. If the service was noteworthy however, then leave the odd change as a tip.

If you leave a large tip where it is not expected, you will brand yourself as an ignorant tourist. By the cut of your clothes and the cut of your hair you are already branded as a tourist. You don't have to open your mouth to prove it. Waiters tend to be multilingual. Yours will probably address you in English before you have ever opened your mouth. Ok. You are a tourist. Don't be an ignorant one.

Chicken under the menu

Jerry and Mary had an interesting dining experience in Vezelay, a medieval pilgrimage town in Burgundy. Encountering pinball machines in the lobby, they feared the place might be a mistake. But inside, it was something else. It was as if they had stumbled into the Middle Ages. There was an earthen floor, rustic tables, a fireplace you could stand inside, and not only were there the ever-present dogs, but there were chickens. They pecked away at the food that had fallen to the floor. The food and the wine were local, home made, cheap and excellent. They did not order chicken.

Dogs

What on earth do dogs have to do with eating? In some European countries dogs are as welcome in a restaurant as people, more welcome than children. I have seen the owner's dog lying under a table in some village restaurants. I have seen a dog served its own meal at the feet of its masters. I have seen a dog in a Belgian restaurant sitting on a seat and eating from a bowl on the table. I have seen a Frenchman feeding a croissant to two dogs sitting on either side of him on a tavern bench while he and we drank our coffee.

Snacks

If you want late night snacks or have a sweet tooth, you can easily satisfy your urges in Europe. All countries seem to have good chocolate, and all have their own type of candies. Cookies come in styles that are unusual for us. I have never eaten one that I didn't like. You can buy potato chips or other types of crunchies. The one thing that is rather difficult to find is popcorn, even at movies.

Speaking of cookies, we should talk a bit more about pastries in general They look beautiful everywhere, but taste accordingly only in France and Luxembourg. The Belgians manage to make them taste like cardboard. Other countries make only a fair imitation of the true French pastries. Have you ever tried a genuine "mille feuille?" It is the French name for what we call a napoleon. Delicious, but gooey. Oh yes, the Italians have great ice cream and tiramisu.

Chapter 10
Water Closet

I gotta go, but where?
One of the most worrisome things about traveling in a foreign country is finding a toilet when you need one. This is especially true when you realize that Montezuma's revenge can strike at any time. Some of the obvious questions are:
- Where can I find toilet facilities?
- Will they be clean?
- Will they have paper and washing facilities?
- Will they be coeducational?

To put your mind a bit at rest, you can almost certainly avoid diarrhea. To put your mind even more at rest, the answers to the above questions are:
- About anywhere.
- Most likely, especially if you go to a respectable facility.
- Most likely, but there are exceptions.
- Occasionally, but even then there is privacy in the stalls.

Now to be more specific, consider that the Europeans eat like we do. They move around like we do. Therefore, they have need of toilet facilities just as we do. Where would you go to look for a toilet in the

United States? Certainly your last choice would be a gas station. Chances are that it would be dirty. It also might be out of toilet paper. Remember the U.S. gas station, and then the options available to you in Europe will be luxurious by comparison.

Multi-flush

We were exploring the Marienplatz in Munich. This is a wide pedestrian and shopping area in the heart of the city. It is best known for the Hofbräuhaus beer hall, and for the animated figures on the clock of the city hall tower. Large crowds gather to watch the figures move when the hour is struck. They only operate twice a day. The best time to watch is 11:00 a.m. For some reason they don't perform at noon.

While we were waiting for the clock to do its thing, Jack mentioned that he needed to find a toilet. I suggested what is always my first choice – a fast food restaurant. There was a Möwenpick nearby, a European chain with very nice facilities for fast sit-down meals. Jack went into the restaurant while I waited outside.

After some time he returned, relieved but excited. It seems that the toilet facilities were very fancy, with many stalls and urinals, patterned tiles on the walls, as well as many wall hangings. Jack decided to take a flash photo of this beautiful room. When the flash went off, all of the bowls flushed in unison. They were operated by an automatic sensor. Jack went spastic. Thank goodness he waited to take the photo until after he had relieved himself.

Customs

Europeans are not as subject to sexual shyness as are we in the U.S. Therefore, you might on occasion find a toilet to be coeducational. Remember that the toilet in your family home is also coeducational, so don't panic. The stalls all have doors on them. The urinals don't, but all men look pretty much the same from the rear. Just pay attention to what you are doing, and let the other people worry about themselves.

Some coeducational toilets must have been built with Americans in mind. They have two separate doors, clearly marked, one for men, and one for women. However, when you go through the appropriate door, you find that there is only one room. Fortunately, it usually has stalls.

All of us travelers have found this sort of toilet in one country or another.

But seriously, you could travel for weeks and never encounter a toilet facility that would expose you to any sexual embarrassment. You will, however, find that toilets in public places often have a female attendant on duty. She is sometimes to be found cleaning the toilets and sinks. People come and go while she is doing this. It is no big deal. She is concerned with the cleaning, and the customers have other things on their minds. They just ignore one another. Because of this attendant, the toilets are most often sparkling clean, and are well supplied with paper, soap and towels, even at expressway rest stops. When the attendant is not cleaning, she is sitting at a table by the door to the toilet. There is a small dish of coins on the table. The idea is that you are expected to put a small tip in the dish as you leave to repay the courtesy of her cleaning services. The customary tip is a coin or two in an amount equivalent to about ten to twenty cents. Always carry some small coins with you to avoid being a free-loader. Besides, at some facilities you are expected to pay before you are allowed into the toilet. This is true, for example, in the toilet facilities at Mont St. Michel in France. Sometimes, but rarely, there is no paper by the stool, and you will only be given paper after you pay. A good reason, in this case, to pay first. That is, unless your wallet is full of small bills. I well remember a toilet in a beautiful public building in Tashkent (not Europe) with no paper at all. Remember that little packet of paper that you put in your suitcase?

Types of toilets

If you are at a private home or in a small family restaurant, you will find a toilet room similar to the one in your home. It is coeducational, but only has room for one person. No problem. Oh yes, there is a problem if you are unprepared. Actually, there are two problems. The first is that there is no sink in the toilet room in a private home. Yes, they do wash their hands. You will find another room just beside the toilet room. This one has a sink and everything you need to restore your hands to a properly sanitary condition.

The second problem is at the toilet itself. There are fewer plumbing standards in Europe than there are in the U.S. The flushing devices come in a wide variety. One of the things that gives Nancy a lot of enjoyment is discovering new flushing mechanisms. Sometimes it is a handle at the side of the tank, just like the ones we are familiar with. Sometimes it is a button on top of the tank at the side. It must be pushed. Sometimes it is a sort of plunger at the top of the tank in the middle. It must be lifted. Sometimes it is a chain behind the toilet that must be pulled. Sometimes it is a knob that you have to turn, like an outside faucet handle in the States. Ed found a toilet in Italy with a button on the wall at least four feet above the toilet. It had to be vigorously pushed several times to operate the flushing mechanism. And Ed is a bit on the short side. Fortunately this engineering and acrobatic challenge can be enjoyed at your leisure after you have taken care of more urgent business. In the British Isles the toilets have a handle that is similar to our toilets, but like the one Ed found, it must be "double-pumped." Sort of like a mouse button on your computer.

Oh yes, on occasion you might find a really old fashioned toilet. In a nice Paris restaurant I once found myself using an oriental-style toilet. It consisted of two rubber foot pads on either side of a porcelain hole in the floor. Surprisingly, I didn't notice any claw marks on the walls. Maybe the French are more supple than I am.

In a public toilet with multiple facilities, the sinks are at the side, just as in the U.S. The urinals, however, might be just a long tin trough with a little running water to dispel odors. Other than that, cleanliness is a byword in most toilets. Make sure you know how to turn on the water in the sink before soaping your hands.

Turkish style

Ed and April were traveling in Germany, and had booked into a hotel in Nürnberg for the night. Each floor had a community toilet at the end of the hallway. Most of the other occupants of the hotel were a group of Turks, on tour. In the morning, while Ed was walking down the hallway, toward the toilet, the door swung open to reveal one of the Turks with a foot on either side of the western-style toilet, squatting above it. He obviously found the western style toilet as objectionable and inconvenient, and perhaps as incomprehensible, as we find his.

Collecting flushing devices

People collect many strange things. My wife, Nancy, has one of the strangest collections in the world. She collects toilet flushing devices. It is quite inexpensive, since she doesn't buy them or carry them home. She merely discovers them. Once we had stopped for a call of nature at a rest stop on the expressway in Switzerland. Nancy and June were in neighboring stalls. Suddenly Nancy called out excitedly, "I've found a new one!" She reached forward to pull a handle on the wall – and the window opened.

Where to find one?

You can find toilets in about the same places in Europe as you do in the United States. Wide experience has given me a priority of choice. The first is a fast food restaurant. The toilet is usually clean, and there is nobody from whom you have to ask permission or directions.

The next choices are not ranked in any degree of desirability. It is just a matter of which you find first. They are a rest stop on the expressway, a public building such as a museum or a city hall, and a large hotel.

The last choices are a store, or a coffee shop or bar. You usually need to look like a customer to use the facilities with minimal embarrassment. However, these places have a distinct advantage. The toilet is often in an unusual location, such as in a medieval basement. The flushing mechanism is also more likely to be unusual and challenging. If you don't feel a great physical urgency, you might enjoy the exploration and the adventure.

A rather unusual, and quite satisfactory toilet is beginning to appear on French street corners. It is an oval concrete structure with a door at one end. The door rolls back to allow a person to enter after putting two francs into a coin slot. The walls and the stool are wet but clean, because the facility has an automatic washing device that operates each time a customer leaves. The idea seems repugnant at first blush. It is a great idea when you have need. Did you remember the coin purse?

The two franc shower
Once, when the older son of Jacques and Michèle was out with the boys, they found need to use one of the two-franc toilets on a street corner. When the last one was leaving, Olivier held the door open and stated his intention of learning how the self-cleaning mechanism worked. He stepped inside, and the door rolled shut. The lads on the sidewalk heard great shouts of distress, but there was no way to open the door until the cleaning cycle had finished. Finally the cleaning came to an end. It took two francs to release the prisoner, who was as wet as if he had fallen into the river. Sometimes education is hazardous.

How to identify one
Toilets can be identified by any of three different visual methods, and like here at home, occasionally by an olfactory method. Some doors, like in the U.S., have a simple sign with the word "MEN" or "WOMEN" in the local language. Since Europeans in tourist areas are accustomed to having visitors who aren't fluent in their language, they tend to make signs international. The doors are often marked with an icon of a man or a woman. You also want to be on the lookout for a sign that says "WC." It stands for the British expression for toilet (no, not "loo") – water closet. If you follow the WC sign you will be going in the right direction. The door to the room will probably have one of the other types of sign.

Men versus women
James, the youngest son of Ed and April, at the age of seven, headed off to the toilet in a very German restaurant. He found the words "Herren" and "Damen" (men and women, that is) on the doors. He immediately went into the "Damen" room, to his embarrassment and mortification. As he explained it to his parents later, "Herren" was clearly intended for several "hers," while "Damen" was just as clearly derived from that Chicago expression "Da Bulls," as in "Da Men." Obviously James' logical skills were outstanding, while his language skills were yet to be fully developed.

Small towns

Small towns offer fewer and less sophisticated facilities than do large cities. Your choices are usually limited to a grocery store or bakery, or to the ever-present sidewalk cafe. I usually choose the latter. To be fair to the owner, I order a coffee or an aperitif and sit a while to watch the local scene. This is one of the great charms of a small town. Relax. Enjoy the scenery. Talk with the other customers. You will be amazed at how much you can learn about local customs.

How to find water

I well remember the time that I used the toilet in the monastery museum at Cluny in France. It is a charming city, by the way. The museum is first rate, and the excavations of the monastery are masterfully done – led by a retired American architect. The original church was the largest in the world in its day. Even today, only St. Peter's Basilica in Rome is larger. Most of the monastery and almost all of the church except for one massive tower were destroyed after the 1789 revolution. The structures were dismantled so that the stone could be used for other buildings.

Anyway, back to the toilet. Nancy and I were in the museum with Jack and June. We all needed to use the facilities. I was the last of the four. As I stepped out of the stall and up to the sink, I saw the other three watching me through the open door. I thought that it was unusual for them to be acting in such a crude manner. I soon realized that they were eager to see how long it took me to discover how to get water at the sink. As I recall, it took me some time – while they giggled – to discover that the water tap was operated by stepping on a button on the floor in front of the sink. I have never been known for my powers of observation.

Emergencies

On occasion, hopefully seldom, you might have an emergency on a back road. It is wise to carry a small packet of toilet tissue with you for these rare occasions or for when the local facility is without paper. Even the best of families in Europe will stop the car and use the roadsides in an emergency.

Chapter 11
The Best Things in Life Are Free

Tourist advice

One of the best and most inexpensive things that you can find in Europe is free advice about what to see and do. The best single source is the host of a bed and breakfast at the time you are eating breakfast. Almost as good a source is the concierge, desk clerk, or management of the hotel that you are staying in at the moment. They rely on tourists for a significant portion of their annual income. It is in their best interest to keep the customer happy. A few minutes of conversation and advice costs them nothing. Besides, if you find the advice worthwhile, you might decide to stay an extra night or two in order to explore further. The next best source of advice is a guest at the hotel where you are staying, or a diner at a neighboring table. People love to share the things that they enjoy. The concierge is also an excellent source for things such as tickets, tours, reservations, cabs and directions. The whole job of the concierge is helping the guests.

Probably the poorest source of advice (this will be hotly contested in some quarters) is a tourist office. Everyone who has a would-be tourist attraction provides glossy literature to the local tourist office. The descriptive text in the flier is equally glossy. After all, the intent is to attract you. I am not advising that you ignore tourist offices. I am saying that you want to read the tourist literature with a skeptical eye. Like many other facets of Europe, this has its parallel in the United States. Now that I have said this, I must compliment tourist offices for their help to the tourists in finding lodging.

How do you tell good advice from poor advice? First of all, you try to judge the sincerity and motivation of the person giving the advice. If there is no obvious benefit to the advisor, the recommendation should be given due consideration. If you have a long enough chat with the person to gain an insight into personality and interests, you can better evaluate the advice.

Here is an example of a bit of free advice that paid off very well. We were staying in a charming bed and breakfast near Mont St. Michel. Most of the guests were gathered in the parlor for a chat in the evening. Some of them were there to attend a large open-air sale of WWII memorabilia. They were much interested in history and local art. When they found out that we were going to Lisieux the next day, they insisted that we make a slight detour to visit the village of Villedieu-les-Poêles. They couldn't seem to make us understand exactly why the village was worth a visit, probably due to our limited command of French and their absolute lack of English. Because they were so interesting and so enthusiastic, we made the detour. It turns out that the word "poêle" means frying pan. The cottage industries of the village specialize in copper, brass and tin products. There is shop after shop with incredible bargains in new items, some of them copies of antiques. One could easily fit out a kitchen with beautiful pots, pans, and measuring cups and spoons. The only negative is that you have carry all of that heavy stuff home. If this is your sort of thing, and it certainly is ours, always ask at the hotel if there are any local crafts, or farmers markets or flee markets.

Sometimes along the roads, both in and out of town, you will see a white sign with the letter *i*. This *i* means information. The sign indicates an unofficial tourist office. These are convenient places from which to learn about the local attractions. However, I have frequently found that I could not locate the tourist office without the help of a seeing eye dog. Sometimes it is no more than the lobby of a small hotel, or the wall next to the door of a grocery. These are the places that tend to have racks of glossy fliers.

Rudeness

Jerry says that the only rudeness they ever encountered in France came from a tourist clerk at a small office near the Church of the Madeleine in Paris. The man simply ignored them. But a Parisian lady who happened to be there unleashed a withering verbal assault upon the clerk for his abominable treatment of them. They missed the choice nuances of her diatribe, but recognized that he was being roundly cussed out.

Road signs

Road signs often carry graphic images of points of interest. If the sign looks good to you, stop for a visit. If you see a castle or a beautiful old church on a hilltop, drive over to take a look. Sometimes the building will not be open to the public, but even so, the close-up view will be worthwhile. The view of the countryside from the top of the hill will often be dramatic.

This subject can also be best illustrated by an example. We were traveling south from Paris toward Lyon. One of the signs on the expressway showed a picture of a large stone building with what looked like a multicolored tile roof. The name of the city was Beaune, the place where all of the nouveau beaujolais wine comes from every November. That seemed to us to be two excellent reasons for taking a break from expressway driving. As usual, we headed for the center of the town. There we found a beautiful building, just like the one in the sign. It was a hospital that had been founded about 500 years ago to care for the poor. It operated until the middle of the 20th century when a more modern facility was built. The old hospital had been staffed by an order of nuns, who maintained it with great love. Now it is a museum showing how the hospital functioned. The chapel, beds (in the chapel), kitchen and pharmacy were carefully restored and furnished. In one hall there is a medieval painting of the last judgement, done on nine panels of wood. It is extremely detailed and finely painted. In my opinion, these treasures are not given due credit in the travel guides.

Stop and smell the roses

Here is another story about flexibility by Ed.

"One of our favorite ways of making a short trip is to just pick a small community and go there. That once took us to Limburg, Germany where we expected to find cheese, but discovered incredibly wonderful baked goods, as well as a magnificent view on the bluffs over the Lahn river. It also took us to Vezelay, France, which sits in the middle of the Burgundy wine region. The village is on top of a plateau that overlooks the entire valley, and is dominated by a large, and magnificent old church. The food and hospitality were 'incroyable.' By going to the smaller communities you experience the real food of a place, and the real people as well. Because they don't see many tourists, they are far more interested in you, and are more interesting to you."

Scenery

It never costs to look at the scenery. Europe has been well blessed by God with a wealth of beautiful vistas. The sights are not as dramatic as some in our own country. Nowhere is there anything like the Grand Canyon, Yosemite, Niagra Falls, or Big Sur. But, canyons, mountains, and seacoasts are plentiful. They are also closer together. When the map says that you are in an area that is scenic, leave the expressway and take to the country roads. You will be well rewarded. Most of the best views, instead of being tourist traps, are in isolated areas with only a tiny village or two nearby.

In Portugal we followed some small signs to the site of a megalithic cromlech, a sort of chapel or tomb made from huge stones set on end. It was located in a farmer's field. We had to drive through the farmyard and around a cow to get to it.

Topless beaches

If your taste in natural beauty includes the human body, then you can view a lot of free sights on the beaches of the Mediterranean coast. Some beaches are dedicated to topless or totally nude sunbathing. Almost all beaches allow "discreet" topless bathers, who can even be found on the banks of the Seine in the heart of Paris.

We were driving along the coast road on the way to Monaco. Naturally, the conversation turned to topless bathing. Now it became like bird watching. First one, then another of us would cry, "There's one!" Jack could never follow the pointed finger quickly enough to spot the sun bird. He began to believe that we were teasing him. We began to believe that he needed a new prescription for his glasses. Needless to say, we had a good time abusing one another.

John and Margie report that on a beach in Portugal they saw the backside of a male bather whom they describe as "bottomless." My own research on the Mediterranean beaches near Malaga, Spain suggests that the older and more overweight a woman, the more she is apt to go topless on a beach. To each his own.

Cities

Most cities have an old town, a medieval area of narrow streets and old stone walls. These areas are often located near a stream with paths, gardens and park benches. Promenades are a favorite form of activity for Europeans before or after dinner. Try it a few times, and you will quickly understand why.

The medieval cities of Avignon in France, Avila in Spain, and Rothenburg in Germany are open to the public without charge. You don't even have to pay for parking. Of course, if you want to tour some of the museums or the better preserved buildings, you will have to pay a modest fee. I have never been disappointed.

Ed tells me that brewery tours in the large cities are often free, and provide all sorts of goodies at the end. He says that he has visited the Heineken brewery in Amsterdam, the Carlsburg brewery in Copenhagen, the Guinness brewery in Dublin, the Kronenberg brewery in Saarbrücken, and the Pilsener Urquell brewery in Plzen in the Czech Republic to name a few. I'll have to tell him the wonders of Diekirch beer in Luxembourg.

Almost all churches are free to the public, sometimes even with guided tours. The only thing asked of you is to respect the sanctity of the place and to keep your voice down for the sake of the worshipers. Churches are not only interesting for their architecture, but they are veritable art galleries. One of the very few churches that I know of where you have to pay admission is the Sainte Chapelle in Paris. It is no longer an operating church, but is maintained as a jewel of Gothic architecture. Until you have seen it, you can have no real appreciation of how refined the arts of carved stone and stained glass became in the 13th and 14th centuries. Often a church will have a crypt or a museum filled with old monuments, art treasures, vestments, and altar pieces. There is usually a small charge for admission. Sometimes you are permitted to climb to the top of a church tower, usually up a circular stone staircase. This too is subject to a small charge. Well worth the price. Once. Not for the claustrophobic.

Flexibility

Here is a story in Jerry's own words that illustrates how important it is to be flexible, and to follow intriguing signs.

"One rainy spring day we were driving along the Circuit des Souvenirs, the road that runs through those sad little English cemeteries, and the trenches and monuments from the 1916 Battle of the Somme. Mary kept seeing posters on telephone poles advertising a new Museum of the Somme that was opening that day in Longueval. She insisted that we stop. And there it was, located in a garish place called the Calypso Bar and Grill. It didn't look hopeful. But we went in and were warmly welcomed as the first American visitors by the owner, Dominic Zanardi, who spoke excellent English. He led us through the tavern to the back yard, which had been converted into a remarkable replica of trenches along the Western Front — muddy dugouts, lookout posts, rusted guns, helmets and shell casings. And when we left, he gave us four balls of shrapnel he had collected from the battlefield. They are now in a display case in our family room — a priceless memo of an adventure that happened as a result of being flexible."

Cemeteries

One of the most interesting things in a city is the cemetery. No, I am not being morbid. Because of the long history of Christianity in most of western Europe, the dead are especially honored and remembered. Cemeteries are carefully maintained. The graves are often covered with flowering plants. You can hardly visit a cemetery without seeing a number of people tending the graves of their family. The tombstones and monuments also vary from country to country, reflecting the local culture. A cemetery is well worth a promenade. Consider three examples that should make my point.

In Vienna there is a large public cemetery. The people seem to be buried by profession. There is an area with a number of tombs honoring engineers. Another area honors explorers. A third is known as Composers' Corner. It has huge monuments to Bach, Beethoven, Mozart, Brahms and the Strausses. You can almost hear the music as you stand amid the beautiful monuments. No bad jokes about decomposing, please.

In Dachau there is a beautiful cemetery on the opposite side of the town from the notorious concentration camp. It is in a heavily treed area. The graves are well shaded, and the light is somewhat dim, even during the day. Each grave has a carved wooden candle holder. In the evenings the candles are lighted. Instead of being ghostly, the effect is peaceful and reverent.

Due to the two world wars, Europe has more than its share of cemeteries to fallen warriors. These are often places of exceptional beauty: in the landscape where they are located, in the immaculate maintenance of the lawns and gardens, and in the monuments and historical plaques which describe the particular battles that resulted in the need for the cemetery. I well remember a drizzly, overcast day when I was walking through an American cemetery in Lorraine. It was full of solemn, respectful visitors – most of them not Americans, but Frenchmen. Don't ever let anyone tell you that the efforts of our troops were not appreciated.

Jerry wants to add a cemetery of his own. He reports that the Cimetière Père Lachaise in Paris is worth a special stop. One passes along little cobblestone lanes beneath horse chestnut trees. There are remarkable sculptures and the graves of famous people – Chopin, Abelard and Heloise, Sarah Bernhardt, Edith Piaf, Bizet, and scores more. It seems to me that if you aren't into history already, such a stroll would definitely be a motivator.

National monuments

Some of the most revered national monuments are open to the public free of charge. I have visited many national memorials to unknown soldiers. The public has free access to all of them. St. Peter's

Basilica in Rome and St. Paul Cathedral in London have free admittance, although, like in many other churches, there are signs that offer you an opportunity to make a donation before leaving. No pressure of any kind.

At the risk of sounding morbid, I must tell you of one more national monument that stands out in my memory. It is the concentration camp at Dachau, just to the north of Munich. Dachau is a beautiful old town that is embarrassed by the horror that happened on its outskirts. A large munitions factory had been shut down as a result of the treaty ending WWI. After Hitler came to power, he reopened the site as a concentration camp, not for Jews, but for political enemies. Thousands lost their lives there. High walls shut the area from public view. Despite this, many people in the city became aware of what was happening and tried to help the prisoners, endangering their own lives. The camp is not advertised as a tourist site in the city, but anyone will direct you to it if you ask. It is maintained as a museum lest we ever forget what can happen when power is abused. Entry is free. You do pay, however with a deep sense of sadness at some men's inhumanity to other men. Who ever said that all education and experience has to be joyful?

Music

Many cities and villages have evening concerts in parks. Many churches, particularly in Austria, offer concerts by visiting choirs and orchestras. In Vienna and Salzburg it is easy to find a church that features visiting musicians at Sunday services. All of these are free. Most of them are excellent, since the competition for permission to perform is intense. Four examples should make my point.

One Saturday in Vienna we saw a sign on the wall of the Augustiner Church, telling that a group would be performing Mozart's Coronation Mass at the 10:00 a.m. Mass the next day. We made sure to arrive early. The church became sufficiently crowded to give a fire marshal a stroke. The music was glorious. It made me quite aware that Mozart had written the music to be performed in just such a building.

On another Sunday we heard a Palestrina Mass at the cathedral in Colmar in the Alsace area of France. It was another example of a marvelous piece of music being performed in the type of building for which it had been intended.

We once spent a delightful afternoon in a park in Vienna. A small group was playing Strauss waltzes in a pavilion. This was not quite free, since we sat at an outside table of a restaurant and nursed a drink. A bargain. The group was not as musically talented as it should be to play Strauss, but it was a great way to rest the feet and enjoy the world around us.

Finally there was another "concert" that was free for the price of a drink and/or a meal. We visited the famous Hofbräuhaus in Munich. The food and beer were excellent, especially since the beer came in two-liter steins. There was an "oomp pah" band that played with enthusiasm in the center of the large hall. It was hard to keep from dancing. Two liters of beer in the belly does, however, help reduce the urge to move the feet. There was a tiny old lady at a table near us. She was well into her second stein (or third) when we left. I don't think she could move anything except her right elbow.

A bargain outing

Ed reminds us that in most major cities the cultural museums are free of charge on Sunday afternoons. In their younger days, Ed and April lived in Brussels on a rather limited income, so they were more informed on bargains than the average traveler. Here is one of his stories.

"Paris is a three hour train ride from Brussels. We would catch the 7:00 a.m. train from the central station, arriving in Paris at 10:00 a.m. with plenty of time to make it to Mass at Notre Dame Cathedral with the children's choir. After Mass it was straight to the Louvre, which opened at noon and was free of charge. After a few hours with Mona Lisa (editor's note: I prefer Winged Victory of Samothrace) we would catch the 4:30 p.m. train and eat a big dinner at home after fasting all day. The cost – $24. For two round trip second class train tickets."

Parks

Public parks are everywhere. They are always free. Most often they have paths, gardens, fountains, ponds, statuary and benches. They also have little booths where you can buy something to eat and drink.

The people watching is great. Parents and nannies bring little boys and girls to sail boats in the ponds. Some people sleep. Lovers spoon. Artists paint. Walkers walk, and lookers look. Tourists sit on the benches and rest their weary feet – and look.

The Luxembourg Garden and the Tuileries Gardens in Paris are free to the walker. The same is true of the Mirabelle Garden in Salzburg, Austria. Even at some of the Loire chateaux that charge for admission to the buildings, a tour of the gardens is open to all comers.

The open spaces in front of some public buildings are also treated like parks. People sit and have lunch, watch their children, walk their dogs, and do most of the things that people do in parks. These squares also attract street entertainers. One can hear excellent music from all over the world. There are mimes and jugglers, and people who make things out of balloons. Remember though, these people rely on tips to make a living. If you like what you see or hear, be kind.

Living statue

Nancy and I were walking in the Tuileries Gardens in Paris. There was a temporary display of statues spaced along the path. We noticed one statue that was a startling white. Italian marble?

As we approached, we saw that the "statue" was a Roman senator. It was actually a young man in a crewcut, dressed in a white toga, head and hands chalky white with body paint. He stood motionless on a wooden box. At his feet was a box. On the box was a cap with a few coins and a sign that said "for the maintenance of the statue." We laughed and discussed the creativity of the young man. No reaction from him. We spoke to him and made faces at him. No reaction. Finally, I threw several small coins into the cap. His right ear rose about half an inch and then quickly settled back into place. More laughter from us. No reaction from him.

Other people gathered around to see what was entertaining those crazy Americans so much. They too found that the statue thoroughly ignored them. I urged them to throw some coins in the cap. As we left we could hear tinkle-laugh, tinkle-laugh. I wonder if there is any money to be made as a statue's agent?

Second best isn't always bad

We were in the southern part of Spain, on our way to tour Portugal. At our hotel we ran into an Englishman who was traveling the reverse direction with his wife. We compared notes on our experiences. He raved about a hotel they had stayed in at Montemor-o-Novo in Portugal. He said that the room, the food, and the service were all excellent. Looking for the town on a map, I realized that it was very close to Evora, a city we had planned to visit. Of course, we decided to stay a night at Montemor-o-Novo rather than at Evora.

We found the hotel to be quite good, but not outstanding, since we had been fortunate in our choice of lodging to date. There was not much to do in the little town, except to visit a small local museum. The museum was closed, but the lady in charge opened it and gave us a private tour. At the end of the tour she played a video that described the countryside. We learned that there were neolithic monuments between this town and Evora. Of course, we explored them and even had a picnic among the obelisks. We might not have found them if we had gone directly to Evora.

Tours

I know, you are going to say I am a hypocrite if I advise taking a tour. I hope not. Tours have their place.

In many cities you can pick up literature for self-guided tours of historic and cultural sites. If you want to know more than you can get from the self-guided tour, you can break down and take a guided tour. Of course, this is not free, but it is advisable if you want to learn more about the history of the city than you have time to do by yourself. Such tours come in a variety of forms – bus tours, horse and buggy tours, boat tours, and lecture tours through a single building. I know, these tours are not free, but I had to talk about them somewhere. The nice thing about them is that you don't have to listen to lectures for days on end, but only for a few hours – and then only on something of your choosing.

Stammtisch Willi

Nancy, Jack, June and I were looking for a hotel for our first night in Salzburg. We found a nice looking place on the edge of town. As usual, I was delegated to do the negotiation. That was really no more difficult than finding out if two double rooms with bath or shower were available, reasonably priced, and clean.

As is customary in a small facility, the hotel clerk and the bartender were a single person at a single counter. I asked my questions in very basic German, and smiled at a group of people sipping beer at a nearby table. After the lady had given me the keys to our rooms, the group invited me to the table, the "stammtisch" and ordered me a beer. I learned that the "stammtisch" is a table set aside for regular patrons, and that I was honored by being invited. One of the regulars, Willi, had visited the States and dearly wanted to show us Salzburg. We couldn't disappoint him, but wondered what he really wanted. In three days, we learned. He just wanted to talk with Americans, brush up on his English, and show off his home town. We saw a part of Salzburg that the average tourist never hears about.

Senior discounts

As long as I allowed some "for fee" topics into this chapter, I might as well talk a bit about senior discounts. Many of the museums and public buildings that charge entrance fees now offer significant discounts to senior citizens. Like us, the Europeans are not of a single mind about when "senior" status begins. It is usually 55 or 62 years. Look carefully at the sign that tells you the entrance fees. If you don't see anything that says senior discount to you, ask the ticket clerk. Most of them speak enough English to handle that question adequately. Be prepared to show your passport to prove your age. Don't feel wounded if you are refused a discount. In some places it only applies to citizens of that country.

People

Yes, Europe has a lot of great scenery, fascinating history, beautiful buildings, churches, castles, monuments and parks. But still, the most fascinating thing that God ever made is man. Be sure to visit with a few people. The results will be rewarding.

If you eat in a small restaurant or stay in a small hotel, you will find the management generally sociable and willing to take the time to talk to you. If you have a snack or a drink at a sidewalk cafe or in a park, the people at a neighboring table will often be willing to exchange courtesies.

In the smaller villages, shopkeepers are usually quite friendly. You can learn more about the history and culture of a place from these people than you can from a guided tour. What you hear might not be quite as accurate as the story told by a professional guide, but it will be far more interesting and colorful.

The palsied hardware clerk

We were in the charming and historic village of Cluny, described earlier in this book. Nancy had spotted some brass trivets in the window of a hardware store. She decided that she needed two of them as presents for friends back home. We entered the store and paid the clerk for the trivets. Like any good French store clerk, he asked if we wished to have them gift wrapped. Sure. Good idea.

We quickly learned that the hardware clerk wasn't talented at wrapping gifts. His fingers were not exactly nimble or gentle. In her best French, Nancy commented, "Vous avez besoin d'une femme." Her intent was to say, "You have need of a woman helper." He heard, "You have need of a wife." Boy, did his fingers shake after that! If she had bought a knife, he would have amputated a finger.

Chapter 12
Experience Your Roots

Where they lived

Your ancestors lived in a different world from the one in which you live. It is hard to imagine what their life was like unless you visit their homeland and personally experience the locale where they lived. If your ancestors were like most immigrants, they came to a New World landscape that resembled what they knew at home. The Scandinavians preferred Minnesota and the Dakotas where the climate was similar to their homeland. The Scots and Irish settled in Appalachia where there were chains of low mountains. The Luxembourgers settled in the Midwest where the gently rolling land was fertile and heavily forested.

Other parts of your ancestors' environment were the villages and cities where they lived, their houses and property, their neighbors, their social activities, church and marketing. Their government had a great impact on them, in some areas forcing them to emigrate.

The landscape

Drive through the countryside on the back roads. Explore the valleys, stop and walk along streams and up the hillsides. From the tops of hills you might be able to see how close the small farming villages are to one another. Look at the fields and the vineyards. See what crops are growing and how they are cultivated. Explore a castle or two and a few manor houses. This, except for the castles and manor houses, is what your ancestors looked for when they came to the New World.

The village and city

There is no better way of experiencing your roots than by walking in the steps of your ancestors – literally. If you can find where they lived, then stroll the streets that they strolled. They probably have changed little. If your ancestors came from peasant farming stock, you will be strolling lanes in a country village. Don't just walk during the day, do so in the evening and on into the late evening. You will meet some of the local people and will find a new dimension of charm.

Farming

Farmers tended to build their living quarters beside or above the animal stalls, in the same building. The animals provided a modest heat supply during the cold winter months. Of course, they also provided abundant odors. Those barn-house combinations are still standing, and are still used in the same way. Some of them are well over 300 years old. Today there might be a tractor in the barn side, but there might also still be livestock.

The barn-houses are grouped in villages of ten to thirty families, spread over the countryside. Each village is surrounded by small fields and pastures. Next to some of the barns you can see, and smell, piles of manure waiting to be spread on the fields. A large pile of manure was a sign of wealth in the old days.

I have a vivid memory of approaching one of these villages at the same time that a young girl was driving the cattle home to be milked. She had two sticks with which she was guiding the cows, the same technique that was used hundreds of years ago. That shouldn't be too surprising, since cattle don't change like human society does.

In one village I saw an old panel truck that had stopped to sell groceries and small items to the villagers. Except for the "modern" vehicle, the method of delivering essentials to the villages seems to be the same as it was over a hundred years ago. In these small villages you will find no hotels, no groceries, no bakery. There would not be enough trade to support such an enterprise.

Houses

Families of ordinary means lived in two story houses of little or no charm. Style meant little, and practicality ruled. As stated before, farmhouses also served as barns. The houses in the cities might be as much as three stories high, and they are generally placed rather close together. They might have a flower garden in front and a vegetable garden in back. In the old days they would have a chicken coop and a pig or two in the back of the house. In Italy the city houses were, and are, behind high walls.

I saw, and photographed several houses where my ancestors lived. One was the house of a direct ancestor. It still bore the name of the family (not mine) that built it about 300 years ago. I discovered that some cousins of mine were living in the house at the current time. They invited me into their garden and popped the cork on a bottle of wine, while comparing family experiences. The house had a television antenna, but otherwise looked as if it hadn't changed much over the years. The furniture was made of wood, old and heavily carved. The carpets were oriental in style.

Furnishings

Look for a local museum or two. They usually contain furnishings and utensils that show you how your ancestors occupied themselves indoors. Some of the better museums display rooms fully fitted out as if people were living there today. Many of the furnishings and utensils are similar to what you can find in historic museums in this country. However, many of them are quite different.

I was impressed with the refinement of some of the furniture. We tend to think of the rough life of those who established the first settlements in this country. Abraham Lincoln sat at a rough plank table in New Salem, Illinois. His European ancestors probably had nicely carved and finished furniture, unless they were poor.

The beds are interesting, because they are very short, and the mattresses are quite thick, usually stuffed with straw. It would seem that every bed was outfitted with a warming pan. No fire extinguishers in those days either!

In a poor house there would be no pictures on the wall. There might, however, be a crucifix and possibly a piece of decorative needlework.

Church

It is rare to see a country village, no matter how small, without a church. These little shrines are usually kept in beautiful condition. The walls are decorated with pictures and designs. Oil paintings and wooden carvings are usually plentiful. The churches are less well attended than they were in the old days, and the shortage of men is quite apparent. All change is not for the better.

In Luxembourg, the services are interesting, since the country has three languages. The readings are in German, which everyone understands. The songs are in French or Latin, which are more melodic than German. The homily is in Letzbergesh, the national language.

Each village church is surrounded by a cemetery. Usually there are few new graves, since local laws are forcing the development of new cemeteries at a distance from the village. The graves are well maintained. Sometimes they are edged in stone. Sometimes a framed photo of the deceased is fastened to the gravestone. Almost all graves are covered with flowering plants, which are tended daily by the family. In some areas lighted candles are placed on the graves in the evening. It makes for a beautiful, respectful atmosphere.

Ancient roots

If you want to experience how the ancestors of your ancestors lived, explore a medieval town and a castle or two. Of course, most of us didn't descend from the nobility, who occupied the castles and the manor houses. But, these people lived off the labor and services of the peasant ancestors of most of us. Contrast life styles. Walk the streets of the towns. Notice, by the way that the center of the cobblestone streets is depressed to serve as a gutter. Now imagine what ran in that gutter and how it must have smelled. Who ever wanted to live in the "good old days?"

In Luxembourg I visited Weidig, a tiny hamlet consisting of only four farms. Several centuries ago these had been estates with the work being done by peasants. Some of the peasant housing is still standing. This is in the form of long, low stone buildings cut up into small apartments, probably consisting of only one or two rooms. Except for the stone walls, it reminded me of slave quarters in the old South.

In another village, Meysembourg, there is a beautiful manor house that dominates the valley. It now belongs to a member of the royal family of Luxembourg. In the 1800's most of the people in the village emigrated, leaving it nearly deserted. Emigration was their only way of escaping from the extremely heavy taxation laid on them by the then local lord of the manor.

Food

Be sure to eat in some small restaurants. Ask to be served some of the local dishes. These are similar to what your ancestors ate. but are probably served with a bit more flair.

Go to a bakery and buy some of the local breads. If your ancestors were poor farmers, their bread was not made of white, refined wheat flour. They ate a dark bread made of cruder grain. Try a loaf of peasant bread or country bread. Certainly it is more delicious today than it was before the development of improved strains of grain. As you are eating the bread, try to imagine how it would be with particles of stone in it from the milling of the flour.

Markets

Find a local farmers market and stroll the booths. Sample some of the offerings. This is the genuine food of the area. Your ancestors sold their produce at markets such as these. Notice the number of people who are gathered in groups, catching up on the local news. These markets were a major social event in the old days. As a matter of fact, they still are. Your great-grandmother and great-grandfather probably first met one another at such a market – and then looked forward to the next market day so that they could meet again.

Neighbors

If you can find a village where your ancestors lived, talk with the neighbors. If you can't find people in the near vicinity of where your ancestors lived, stop and take some refreshment in a local cafe or pub. Strike up a conversation with several people. Ask them questions. Ask everybody questions. You will be surprised at how much you can learn.

Sources

Rather than blindly wandering about, how can you give some direction and organization to your exploration of your family's way of life? There are several good sources of reference.

Hopefully you have done some reading of history and local culture before you ever leave home on your journey. There is a great series of books by a Frenchman named Fernand Braudel. They were written to study the evolution of economics, and tend to be dry for the average reader. However, if you browse these books carefully, you can find wonderful treasures of information about the lifestyle of your ancestors.

You studied maps before you left home. Do so again when you arrive at the location of your ancestors. Book shops and tourist offices can often provide you with detailed maps of the local area, maps that are not available elsewhere. They will include the location of very small villages not shown on the touring maps.

I recommended visiting a local museum or two. It is worthwhile to visit such museums both before and after your exploration of the area. The first visit will help you to know what to look for. The second visit will enhance and expand the images you have formed.

Chapter 13
Family Research

National archives

National archives are a good place to look for expertise in how to search out details of your ancestry while in the country of your family's origin. If the country is large, you will probably find it impractical to search for specific records. Just make sure that you can get the same records at home in the Family History Center of the Church of Jesus Christ of Latter Day Saints. You spent a lot of money getting to the land of your ancestors. You don't want to waste your time sitting at a microfilm viewing machine to do what you can do at home.

This organization, the Mormon Church, has a vast library of microfilm records of births, baptisms, marriages, deaths and burials. It is much easier to do the detailed searching here at home. But expert advice on what to look for is more available in the old country. Note that in most national archives you can't have access to records that are less than a hundred years old. This is a protection against fraudulent use of identities.

Normally you won't find records of your family before the early 1600's, except in a few villages where pastors kept records before the practice became mandated. If, however, you are descended from royalty, the archives should be able to provide you with a wealth of information about your family.

I made the acquaintance of a researcher in the National Archives of Luxembourg. He listened to my queries and theories as to the roots of my family, and he recommended areas of new research for me. He even gave me several books from the archives, one of them a treasure of information about people who had emigrated in the latter part of the 19th century.

Professional genealogists

A professional genealogist can sometimes give you a lead or two to help you find a way around a dead end in your research. He or she can also help you with a difficult translation, particularly if it involves the name of a person or place. Consider asking a professional genealogist what it would take to find the origin of your family name. It might be easier and less expensive than you think. However, the services of such professionals are generally quite expensive.

I have known a number of people who pay a researcher to do in-depth search for their ancestors. Frankly, I'd advise you to avoid that unless you can find a true professional, and can afford to pay the bill. In my experience, the quality of work from amateur researchers is generally poor. A lot of them find "things" to let you know that they are working, and many tend to do slipshod translation.

Heraldry

If you think that your family might have a coat of arms, or if you want your family to have one, consider visiting a heraldry expert. You are more likely to find a reliable one in an office in Europe than you are at a tourist site in the U.S. Don't be disappointed, however, if there is no coat of arms for your family. My own family is descended from peasants. Of course we have no coat of arms. The closest that I could come to one is the coat of arms of the city of Vitry-sur-Orne, from which my peasant ancestors took their family name.

Local registries

The records in local units of government are kept by the secretary in the local town hall. Sometimes you will be greeted as an unwelcome pest. Sometimes you will be welcomed with open arms. In the latter case you might gain access to things you never dreamed of. Ask, ask, ask. Be sure to ask if there is a local copy of emigration records. People needed a permit, a sort of passport, in order to emigrate.

In this local office you might, just might, be able to obtain a few documents less than a hundred years old. You will need to persuade the clerk (the secretary) that you are directly descended from the person(s) whose records you seek. He might allow you to look at the records but not copy them.

I well remember the town hall of Kayl in Luxembourg. I made the acquaintance of the financial officer. He opened the door for me in other offices and spent a lot of time discussing my area of interest. He pulled out a book of 300-year-old records of baptisms, marriages and interments. I paged through the book, comparing what was there to my own records. The Mormons had copies of everything; there was nothing new. But I was actually handling and reading the original records, on thick, bluish paper. The script was in Latin and rather easy to decipher, so I translated some of the text out loud. Then I commented that I was surprised at being allowed to handle this priceless and fragile book. The answer was that I was quite welcome, since I had more interest in it than did the residents of the town. Oh yes, as I left I was given copies of two local history books. There wasn't much about my family in them, but there was a lot of local color.

Parish records

Before it became a civil function, the recording of births, marriages and deaths was done by the local pastor. He recorded them as baptisms, marriages and interments. Some of these records might have been missed by the Mormons, or were not made available to them because of theological differences.

So, be sure to visit the local parish house and ask about the availability of records. If the pastor is up in years, he can provide a wealth of local color and history, as well as access to local records.

Histories and maps

Whether you are in a town hall or a parish house, ask if there are any maps of the local area, or any local histories. It is amazing what you can find. The maps are usually rather primitive, but often contain information that the commercial maps don't.

Local histories are truly a treasure house. Unfortunately, they are usually written in the vernacular. Of course, if you are a serious genealogist, you will have learned some of that language. You also know how to browse a document to see if your family name shows up.

Mr. Miny of Nommern

One experience with a local history was so rewarding that it deserves a special place in this chapter.

I was in Schrondweiler, Luxembourg, exploring the village where my family started. At least the written record of my family started there. I took some photographs and wandered the village. At one house I asked if anyone in the area was an historian or had ever written a history of the village. I was directed to an old house, surrounded by untended trees and shrubbery.

As I knocked on the door, a large dog vocalized his disapproval of my trespassing. Eventually the owner of the house showed up, but not from inside the house. He came around the corner of the building from the garden. The large knife in his hand gave me a moment's pause, but the bunch of garden vegetables in the other hand reassured me.

The old man told me the general history of the village and then directed me to look for a Mr. Miny in the neighboring village of Nommern. He assured me that Mr. Miny could provide me with a book of local history.

Mr. Miny was easy to find, since he ran a small inn with his name above the door. He ushered me into his parlor after hearing what I was searching for. He rummaged in a bookshelf and came up with a bound volume that was the history of the area. I opened it at random, and found my family name. Upon my request for a copy, Mr. Miny sold me his and told me that the money would go to the local parish. It turned out that the former pastor had written the book because of the frequency with which he was questioned about family roots and local history.

Now for the pièce de resistance. I had developed the theory that my most remote ancestors were a family that was called by the name of Thies, because they had been serfs on the Thies estate. That theory was reinforced when I saw the Thies estate in Schrondweiler. Now it was verified in Mr. Miny's book. The pastor called those people by my family name rather than by the name Thies. I hope you can be so fortunate in your on-site research.

Church records

If you are a purist like me, you might want to look for church records of those people who entered religious life. As I have studied more about the social customs of my ancestors, I have learned that it was quite common for younger sons and daughters to enter religious communities. The driving force, at least for young men, was the custom of selective inheritance of the parents' property by the oldest son. A young man had to have reliable employment or a piece of property in order to be married. Neither was easy to come by for the younger sons.

As a result, many of your aunts, uncles and cousins of past generations simply disappeared from the public records after they were born. If they entered religious life, their records were kept by the local convent, monastery or diocesan office. I intend to look for the records of religious communities in Luxembourg on my next visit.

Libraries

If you want to study old histories, you would be well advised to visit libraries. They tend to keep local histories stored in a common place. Librarians are usually eager to help the researcher.

Maps of a few centuries past will sometimes show the names of villages that no longer exist, or villages whose names have changed. When you are looking at old records, you want to have a map with old names. Obtain a few.

In the national library of Luxembourg I found a number of histories that were no longer available in bookstores. I was welcome to make copies of any pages I wished. At the same library I asked about old maps that showed the area in the 17th through the 19th centuries. I was delighted to find that there was a map expert on the staff – with a roomful of old maps. He made copies of several that seemed to meet my needs. Talk about "hog heaven!"

Cemeteries

In the previous two chapters I encouraged you to browse old cemeteries for their ambiance and to gain a feeling about what your ancestors experienced. Now I have to tell you that European cemeteries are of little value to the average genealogist. The reason is that the burial customs are different from ours. Generally the body is not embalmed, and the caskets are usually made of wood, at least in the farming villages. The burial plot is rented, and not permanently leased or owned permanently. When, after a number of years, there is another death in the family, the grave is opened, the remaining bones are moved to one side, and the new body is interred. The name of the newly deceased is added to the family monument.

If the size of the family declines, the grave site lease is dropped. A new family picks up the lease and puts up its own memorial marker.

The result is that it is difficult to find a gravestone with a date more than a hundred years old. If you do find one, chances are that it marks the grave of someone of noble blood, or it is covered by weeds and has been forgotten over the generations. It will also be difficult to read, since most gravestones were made of a soft limestone that doesn't weather well.

The living are important too

When I was suffering my most severe infection with the genealogy virus, I one day experienced a renaissance. I asked myself if I was more interested in the dead than I was in the living. From that moment I sought out living members of my family in this country as well as in Europe. The results have been quite rewarding.

This year I attended two family reunions in this country, and one in Luxembourg. It was great to meet people who are related to me through ancestors eight generations back. Interestingly, many of the family members in Luxembourg did not know one another before I began my research.

So, do your genealogical thing, but consider looking for the living as well as the dead. The rewards are remarkable.

Interviews

Speaking of the living, you might look for specific living people to help you in your genealogical research. If you have found any villages, or better yet, any houses where your family lived, speak with the neighbors. They might be able to tell you something about your ancestors. Ask if anyone in the locale is interested in genealogy, and then follow up any leads.

Look in the phone book for the addresses of people in the area who have your family name. They might be related. If so, they might be motivated to look for information for you. I have seen such information in the family Bible. I have seen it in family trees hung on the wall. You will never find these things unless you ask.

You will have better luck if your family name is uncommon, as is mine. I wouldn't even try to find living relatives if my family name was Jones or Schmitt or Carlson. As it is, by pursuing these leads from neighbors and people with the same name I have been able to trace a number of previously unknown branches of my family back to the main root. May you have similar success.

Good hunting!.

Chapter 14
Purchases

General rules
In our family we have three general rules about purchases. The first rule is that we are rich, with rich being defined as keeping our yearnings within our earnings. If we don't think that we can afford something, then we can't.

The second rule is not to buy something that we can obtain in the United States. It is usually less expensive at home, and it doesn't have to be carried for five thousand miles.

The third rule is that if we see something that passes the first two rules, and if it is appealing, buy it! I have seen too many people who berated themselves on their return for having passed up something that they might never find again.

The lonesome statue
We had spent a night at a charming old castle in the Loire valley. The castle was almost a thousand years old. Our huge old-fashioned room even had a fireplace. On the mantle was a medieval stone statue of St. Peter, holding the keys to the Church. I complimented our host

and expressed amazement that the statue had never been stolen by a guest. I didn't tell him that I had been sorely tempted.

Later in the trip we were window shopping in Luxembourg City. I saw several statues that were similar to the one in the castle. They were smaller stone reproductions of other medieval statues. The price of these statues was a bit more than I was prepared to spend. I stewed about it for one night and decided in the morning that I would purchase one of them. Naturally, when I managed to return to the shop, it was closed for the mid-day lunch period. There was no time left. We had to leave.

Several years later I returned to Luxembourg. After much searching, I found the store again. It no longer carried the statues. He who hesitates is lost! Thankfully, on a later trip, I managed to find a similar – but not as nice – statue elsewhere. St. Peter is looking down at me now from the shelf over my desk.

Where to shop

Unless you are truly wealthy, the last place to shop is in the exclusive "shoppes." In fact, if you have purchased this book and have read this far, it should demonstrate that you are value conscious and are not overly concerned about brand names just to show how foolishly you can spend your money. For this reason, I recommend that you avoid shopping too much in the fashionable part of any major city. You are likely to pay much more than the value of the object you covet, be it a dress, a purse, a book, or an ice cream cone. You will be paying for the overhead. If you want something affordable with a fancy brand name on it, go to Hong Kong. It won't be expensive, but it won't be genuine either.

If you are shopping for something that you would expect to find in an American department store, then look in a department store in the country that you are visiting. But, if you are shopping in a department store, it means that you are probably looking to obtain something that you should have brought from home in the first place. If Nancy were looking over my shoulder at the time I was writing this, she would object strenuously. She finds department stores excellent places to buy needlework items and what I call "dust catchers." That is, little things that sit on shelves and are seldom useful or used. It seems to me that in a department store the looking is everything and the buying should be limited to rare moments of true inspiration.

In Europe the stores have always specialized. If you need medications, you go to a pharmacy. If you need bakery goods, you go to a bakery. If you "need" jewelry, you go to a jewelry shop.

However, Europe is now following all of the trends in the U.S. This includes malls and stores that don't specialize. You can find stores where you can buy almost anything that the homeowner needs. These are good places to go to buy groceries and grooming materials. They are not good places for finding unique items that represent the local culture and arts.

To find things that represent local culture, you must search for the crafts that are local specialties. These tend to be things that you either can't find at home, or things that are extremely expensive at home. The best sources of information about local crafts are travel guidebooks and chats with local people or experienced travelers. Several examples might help you visualize the sort of things that I am talking about. In the area of Garmisch-Partenkirchen in Bavaria you can still find hand-carved wooden figures at a reasonable price. In Villedieu-les-Poêles in Normandy you can find charming copper and brass items that are styled after antiques. Just to the south of Oporto (Porto) in Portugal you can buy fine porcelain from the factory at incredibly low prices. Of course, it is very heavy and bulky to carry home. There are places to find pewter, crystal, china, paintings, and all sorts of craft items. Some of these can be purchased at home, but they are generally less expensive at the point of production.

Two of the best places to find good buys are a sidewalk sale and a country market. In this case you don't go looking for something special. You just browse to see what is there. If you are having a picnic or are staying in a place with cooking facilities, don't overlook the seasonal specialties in the market, such as white asparagus and wild strawberries. Often you also discover something unusual that you find you can't do without. The prices of items at these sales are either ridiculously low or deceptively high. In the countryside the market vendors move from town to town, each town having its special market day. Two other types of markets deserve special attention – the flea markets and the specialty markets, like the stamp market on the right bank of the Seine in Paris.

Art market

Here is another recommendation from Ed.

"A great thing to do in large cities on Sundays is to go to any of the many markets which operate only on the weekends. There are cheese markets in Holland, and antique markets most everywhere. There are fruit and vegetable markets, and even art markets. Artists come from all over England to display their wares around Hyde Park on Sunday afternoons. We have a beautiful (and cheap) oil painting hanging above our fireplace. It was purchased by the headlights of a lorry, and was carried all over Europe by me. Oh yes, that was my wife's idea."

A few footnotes – editor's privilege. There is a great miscellaneous market at Portobello Street in London on Sundays. You can find everything from vegetables to suits of armor. We too have a cheap, but treasured painting – from a starving artist shop on Montmartre hill in Paris. We also have another treasured painting from a street artist on the Arbat street in Moscow.

Memory items

Hopefully you will visit sites of extraordinary beauty or history. Examples are Notre Dame Cathedral in Paris, Westminster Cathedral in London, the medieval city of Rothenburg in Germany, the prehistoric paintings in the cave at Lascaux in the region of Dordogne in France, and the wind-carved grottos on the southern coast of Portugal. At these places you will find that the tourist shops sell a lot of dust catchers. However, they also sell two things to which you want to give serious consideration – post cards and coffee table books.

Post cards have two uses. The first is to tell your family and friends back home where you are and to tell them that you are thinking about them, poor devils. The second is to take home an image of the things you have seen. You will no doubt take a lot of photographs. However, the light is not always favorable, and you can't always stand at a place that shows the subject in the best perspective. This is particularly true indoors, such as in the large halls in Versailles and in the crypt below the castle of El Escorial where the Spanish royalty are buried. Also, if you are like me, you sometimes have misfires with the camera. For these reasons, you might want to add a few postcards to your photo file. If you send postcards home, make sure you add "U.S.A." at the bottom of the address, and ask the local post office for the proper stamps.

No matter how much research you do in advance, and no matter how carefully you observe a thing of beauty or history, you will walk away with questions. In addition, memories fade over time, and different sights tend to become confused in your mind. "Did I see that in Avignon or in Carcassonne?" For these reasons you might want to keep a daily journal to list the places you visited and the things you experienced. June does this, and we have found the record quite useful when we have our photos developed. You might also consider the purchase of a local coffee table book which describes a place that especially impresses you. If you wait until you are home to decide on a purchase, it will be too late. As an example, our older daughter purchased a book about Salzburg, Austria when she was on a choir tour (ugh, bad word!) She later loaned it to a friend. It was never returned, and she forgot who had it. She grieved over the loss for years. Finally, Nancy and I went to Salzburg ourselves. The only request Mary Beth had was that we bring back a replacement for the lost book. She could even describe it so accurately that I had no trouble picking it out from a variety of such books.

Making a purchase

In many stores, particularly those that specialize in serving the tourist trade, you will be approached by a clerk who will offer to be of service. Don't be surprised if you are addressed in English. Americans stick out like sore thumbs, even if they aren't ugly. If you say that you are just browsing, the clerk will let you alone. If you ask to see something special and can't find it, don't be surprised if the clerk begins to show you alternative items. If you are not interested, make a polite refusal and turn away.

If you are interested in an item, and if the clerk speaks no English, it is now time to show off one of the foreign phrases that you have prepared for. Ask, "How much?" If you look puzzled at the response, the savvy clerk will write the price on a piece of paper. In most of

Europe the price is fixed. In the Mediterranean basin a clerk in a small shop or in a small town might be prepared to haggle a bit. Europe is definitely not like Oriental and Arabic countries where virtually every purchase is expected to be the result of a haggle.

If you decide on a purchase, notice if there is a dish resembling an ash-tray on the counter. If so, you are expected to put the money in the tray. The clerk will then put the change in the same tray for you to pick up. Although this practice seems to be dying out, I have seen clerks who refuse to pass money directly from hand to hand.

In many countries there is a national VAT or value added tax. This is somewhat like our sales tax, except that it is included in the price of the object. The tax in not inconsiderable, being in the range of 12% to 21% of the purchase price. If you purchase something at a very high price, ask for a receipt for it because of the VAT. When you leave the country, you can request a refund at a special desk in the airport. Sometimes the refund is immediate. More often you are given a form to mail back to the appropriate government department. Sound like a rebate?

Store hours

Store hours vary by country and by custom. Stores, except for bakeries, generally open later in the morning than in the U.S. They also tend to close for a midday break of about two hours. Even the groceries and supermarkets tend to close in the middle of the day. If you are planning on a picnic, plan well in advance. Did I mention that one of your first purchases might want to be an inexpensive cooler? Many stores also close on Saturday afternoon and on Sunday. I well remember one Sunday in Geneva, Switzerland. The only things that I could do were to go to church, take a walk, and explore a museum. Everything else was shut tight.

Ed makes an interesting note about a shopping custom in Norway. He says that the people in the countryside are particularly honest. Many stores remain open during the lunch break even though the employees have left. People go in to make a purchase and leave their money on the counter where it remains untouched until the employees return.

Instant rebate

Nancy had returned home, and I had stayed in Europe an extra week to do genealogical research in Luxembourg. I had purchased a number of items, and was given a few presents by members of the family that I discovered. In total, I was loaded with luggage and was about $60 over the $400 customs limit.

I picked up my luggage from the carousel in O'Hare airport in Chicago, and headed for the customs clerk. I held the customs declaration card in my teeth and leaned forward for the clerk to take it. He did. Now that I could speak, I told him that I owed him some money. He glanced at the card and asked, "Do you pay your taxes?" When I assured him that I did, he said, "Consider this a rebate." My kind of customs clerk!

Careful about limits!

It is well to be prudent about what you buy. Make sure that you know what your import limits are at home. There is a limit on the total amount you purchase – $400 at the current time. You are limited to one liter of hard liquor. There are limits on tobacco and a few other items. You can exceed these limits, but you will be expected to pay duty before you leave the customs area of the airport.

Some things cannot be brought home. This includes any animal or vegetable item that might bring with it a disease or a pest. If you bring home food, make sure it is in a tightly sealed commercial container. Don't plan to bring home cheeses from a local market. They are not allowed. Besides, the smell will give you away.

Watch your weight. If you are like me, your waistline will grow a bit in Europe. But this is not the weight I am talking about here. Remember that you have to carry all of the things you buy. On one trip I brought home eight cans of Luxembourg beer. I love it, and it is not available outside Luxembourg. I also brought home fourteen books of French history and classic literature. There were times when I wondered about my sanity. Other times I had no doubt. I pretended to myself that carrying the load would help my waistline. Man is a reasoning animal – if only he would.

Oh yes, cans of beer fit very nicely inside shoes. I do not tell you this to urge you to bring home cans of beer. But, if you have things that fit inside shoes, you can accomplish two things. First, you can avoid consuming excessive suitcase space. Second, you can prevent your shoes from being squashed out of shape.

Who died on the plane?

We were on the plane, returning to the States. Nancy noticed an unpleasant odor that seemed to be growing stronger by the minute. Suddenly several stewardesses began bustling about the cabin, opening overhead compartment doors and sniffing.

One of the stewardesses said something like "aha!" and pulled a shopping bag out of a compartment. She asked who owned it and what it contained. The owner identified himself and showed her a large number of cheeses that he was taking home. They were wrapped only in cellophane. The stewardess wrapped the whole bundle in several layers of heavy plastic bags that had seals. Gradually the odor died away. I have always wondered what happened if the customs agents inspected the man's luggage, or what the cheese might do to the nose of a drug-sniffing dog.

Electronics

There are a number of things that you will want to avoid buying, simply because they are available at home at a more reasonable price. This includes all electronic devices. In case you forget this piece of wisdom, you will be reminded when you gasp at the price tags. I believe it is called sticker shock.

CD's are also very expensive, generally costing from 50% to 100% more than at home. However, they are like the coffee table books. If the CD is of local origin and is an off brand (not Philips,) you will not be able to find it at home. Examples are organ music from cathedrals, local choirs, and folk music. If you find something that you really want, and if you have any doubt about its availability at home, you would do well to buy it. It might be years before you ever visit the same place again.

They cremated my baby

We had been on a trip to the Orient. The agenda included a few days in China. In the garden of a classic old home I found a merchant selling bonsai trees. They were ridiculously inexpensive. I could not withstand the temptation, and purchased one.

I treated that tree with loving care. I carried it in a special bag so that it wouldn't be crushed. Every night I watered it carefully and slowly so that it wouldn't be damaged or dry out. It traveled with us through Hong Kong, Bangkok and Tokyo. Until we came to Hawaii. The customs agent asked if we had any plants or vegetable products. Being chronically honest, I told him about the tree. He grabbed it, held it at arms length, and began to carry it off. I asked what he was going to do with it. His answer: "We'll cremate it."

Chapter 15
Handling Money

Forms of money

How much money will you need on your trip? Only you can answer that question. Only you can estimate how much you will spend. Only God knows what unexpected shopping opportunities you will discover, or what unplanned expenses you might incur. The most important thing is to avoid running out of money.

You can carry money, or access to money, in a variety of ways – cash, travelers checks, bank checks, credit cards, and ATM cards. I usually carry about $100 in cash for use in the airport when leaving and when returning. About $10 of that amount is in one-dollar bills for use as tips in foreign countries if I find myself out of the local currency. I have never seen anyone refuse a banknote as a tip.

Travelers checks aren't too expensive, and are a secure means of carrying money. They are secure if you remember to leave at home a copy of the receipt that identifies the serial numbers of the checks. If your research tells you that money changing facilities are not readily available in your target country, you might want to obtain the travelers checks in that currency. My European friends do this when they travel to the U.S. I personally have never found it to be necessary when traveling abroad. On our last several trips, each of which lasted three weeks, I carried $2000 worth of travelers checks in $100 increments. They were never needed, but they gave me a sense of financial security.

It is prudent to carry a few personal checks and to make sure that your checking account has a reasonable balance. A personal check might come in handy if you find it necessary to buy new airplane tickets because of an unexpected emergency. However, most businesses are reluctant to accept foreign checks. The check writer is usually long gone before the check clears the bank. If the check bounces, the local business is left holding the bag.

A credit card is a very convenient way of paying your bills on your trip. You are usually given the current rate of exchange, and you then have a printed record of what you spent. The reason why you obtain a good rate of exchange with a credit card is that the financial institution that issued the card is exchanging millions of dollars every day for the foreign currency with which you are dealing. This ensures that they obtain a good rate of exchange, which you then participate in.

Not every business will accept a credit card. This is particularly true in Germany where plastic money has only limited acceptance. And that brings up a significant point of caution. Always have on hand enough of the local currency to cover all of the anticipated expenses of the day and the cost of a night's lodging. It is rather embarrassing to have your credit card refused only to discover that you don't have the money available to pay your bill. Or do you like washing dishes in a restaurant?

One of the most convenient uses of a credit card is to pay tolls on expressways. This is faster than waiting for the toll clerk to make change.

If you have several different credit cards, carry them. As in the U.S., some businesses refuse certain types of credit cards.

An ATM card is an extremely useful device for obtaining local currency at a fair rate. The service charge is only $1. All you have to do is find an ATM machine. That is really not too difficult. Look for a bank. Most banks have a machine just inside the front door or on the sidewalk in front of the building. You will also find ATM machines in unexpected locations in large cities. If you don't see a bank, look for a post office. Most ATM machines will offer you a choice of languages. If they do, English is always one of the options. Don't expect an ATM machine to give you more than the equivalent of $300 in the local currency, unless the machine belongs to the bank that issued your ATM card.

A word of caution is appropriate here. On one trip, I found that my ATM card was refused at German banks but was honored at French banks. It turned out that the magnetic strip on the back of the card had a few minor scratches. The German ATM machines were unable to read it, but the French ones had no problem. What is the condition of your ATM and credit cards?

Another word of caution. Best to check well in advance of leaving home to make sure that your ATM card and your credit cards are usable abroad. They might be valid only in the U.S. Check early enough so that you have time to obtain more usable cards in case you find that yours are restricted to domestic use. You would be well advised to carry two different credit cards, just in case.

Romin' thieves

I was on a business trip just before I retired. Nancy wasn't there to keep me out of trouble. I was walking along the Tiber river in Rome when a group of young children came running up to me. One of them, a teenager, kept pushing at my chest with a piece of cardboard while he and the others yelled things at me in a strange tongue. I thought they were begging, since beggars in the Mediterranean basin tend to hold a paper in their hand as they ask for money.

Suddenly I heard something hit the ground, and all of the children ran in different directions. The lad with the cardboard had pushed a wallet out of my coat pocket. This was just what he intended to do. Fortunately it was a book of travelers checks, and not my wallet or passport. The only real loss was to my pride. I learned later – too late – that this was a typical gambit of gypsy children, and that I should have been forceful in driving them away. A word of warning for you other travelers.

Exchanging money

When you exchange cash or travelers checks for local currency, you pay a significant price for the service. You pay a rate of exchange that is less favorable than the market rate. You might also pay a service charge. This can result in paying a premium of up to 10% of the amount of currency that you are exchanging. The best way to avoid this is to avoid exchanging money. Your ATM card and credit cards are the key to this.

With a credit card you do not pay any fees. With an ATM card you pay a dollar per transaction. With both you get a fair market rate of exchange. Be careful, though. Some banks that issue credit cards and ATM cards have begun to add a surcharge of up to 4% for transactions that involve currency exchange. This is being objected to by consumer groups, so it might not affect you. Best, however, to check it out.

There are times when you must exchange money, particularly if your credit card is refused and there is no ATM machine available. In this case, there are two things that you want to avoid. First, avoid paying with greenbacks or travelers checks even though some restaurants and hotels accept them. The rate of exchange will almost certainly be most unfavorable, since the establishment must exchange your dollars for local currency, with significant inconvenience and bank charges for the service. Second, avoid the little kiosks that advertise money exchanging services. Here is where you pay a high service charge as well as an unfavorable exchange rate.

If you must exchange dollars, do so at a bank as your first choice. You will receive a fair exchange and will pay a modest fee. If you are in a small town that doesn't have a bank, go to the post office. It too will give you fair service at a modest fee. The last choice for a reasonably fair exchange rate is a money change booth at the airport. Their fees are usually higher than those at banks. If you exchange money at any of these facilities, they will ask for your passport. They need your passport number when they record the transaction for the government.

Try to avoid exchanging money from one foreign country for that of another. I did that once when I went from France to Luxembourg. You pay twice the penalty, two somewhat unfavorable rates of exchange and two service fees. Not the best transaction in the world. Always try to manage your money so that you leave a country with a minimal amount of the local currency remaining in your wallet.

Currency conventions

If you look at the price of a fancy car in a showroom, you will see a number that looks like 60 750,59dm or 60.750,59dm. Where we write $60,750.59, the European convention is to use different punctuation and sometimes to put the currency symbol behind the number. The conventions differ between countries. In Portugal a price of 350 escudos would be written as 350$00.

How much is a price of 350ff in real money? First of all, French francs *are* real money. Ok, how much is it in dollars? Now that is a fair question. Did you remember to look up the rate of exchange before you left home? If you did, then you now have two choices for how you find the answer. One is to carry a small calculator in your pocket or purse. The other is to do an approximation using a convenient multiplier or divisor. If it takes about 6 French francs to make a dollar, then divide by 6 – giving a price of about $60. The correct answer is really closer to $58 – today. It will change tomorrow. If you need to worry about the difference, you should have stayed home. This approximation technique becomes a bit more tricky when you are in countries with inflated currencies. In Portugal, it takes about 185 escudos to make a dollar. To approximate the dollar equivalent, you would divide a price by 2 and move the decimal point two places to the left. A hotel room at 10,000 escudos is really about $50, or $54 to be more precise.

Don't trust the above exchange rates to be accurate at the time you read this book. Check them before you leave. You can do this in the *Wall Street Journal* or on Internet. If you visit a country that is experiencing galloping inflation, you don't want to exchange money until the last minute, and then only in modest amounts. In such countries you might find that your best exchange rate is from a merchant from whom you are buying something. He will take U.S. currency and give you change in the local currency – at a better rate than a bank.

Coins

Coins are very convenient for a variety of uses. Make sure that you keep your change, and don't spend it too readily to try to keep the weight down in your pocket or purse. Coins come in more denominations than in our country, up to the equivalent of $3 in some countries. These coins are great for parking meters – better than accumulating traffic tickets. They are also great for vending machines, tips, and toll booths where the fee is so small that you don't want to bother with a credit card. Sometimes they are indispensable for the use of a public toilet. There are occasions when you don't have time to look for a bank.

A word of caution about coins. You can exchange paper money for dollars at the end of your trip if you are willing to pay the exchange rate and fee. Nobody will exchange coins.

We had a great time once in a grocery store on the border of Portugal, just south of Spain. We were passing into Spain and were not going to visit Portugal again on that trip. Our common purse held about $5 worth of Portuguese coins and currency. What to buy with it so that it "didn't go to waste?" We bought items for our next picnic. It was funny to see four people running around, selecting items, checking to see if we had exceeded our funds, and putting back things that took us over the limit. As I recall we wound up with a wine that was a cut above what we had been drinking on that trip. Sure enough, the cheese was wrongly priced on the shelf. We had to make the checkout clerk wait while we returned it and selected another cheese. She chuckled at us. I think she knew exactly what we were doing. Crazy Americans.

Purse

If several families are traveling together, it can be convenient to carry a common purse for common expenses. As Jacques says: "Good counts make good friends." There are many common expenses – tolls, gasoline, parking, tips, entry fees, church donations, etc. If the members of the group have similar tastes in food and lodging, even these can be paid for from a common purse.

When we travel with Jack and June, I am the designated treasurer, and carry a small coin purse. Each couple donates equal amounts to the purse to begin the trip, and then refreshes the purse when it begins to lose weight. It is a simple and convenient mechanism by which to handle a myriad of common expenses without the need for keeping books. We only keep a written record of major expenses that are paid for by credit card. The other three do that. Believe me, I have the easier job.

Chapter 16
Telephones

Intimidation
In an earlier chapter I spoke about being intimidated by bus systems. I don't suppose that I am the only person in the world who has a fear of being marooned at the end of a bus line with no obvious way of getting back to where I started. In a way, the telephone is even worse. The first time that you try to use a telephone in a foreign country, you will find out that all of the conventions you were accustomed to at home have gone out the window. This too can be quite intimidating.

But, after a number of trips abroad, I have learned that you can be successful in using the telephone if you go at it with imagination and determination. Remember, it is a device that is supposed to help you communicate. This chapter will not answer all of your questions, but it will give you some helpful hints, and hopefully minimize the intimidation factor.

Finding a public telephone
In cities you can find public telephones in large buildings and on street corners in just about the same frequency as in the U.S. In small

towns there might be only one or two public telephone booths, usually on street corners near the town square. If you are in a village so small that there is no public telephone booth, go to the post office. In most countries the telephone and postal service come under a single governmental agency. The post office in a small village usually offers telephone services and even limited banking service.

The telephone thief

We were in a small village in Austria, not far from the German border. It was the time of day when it would be possible for Nancy to reach her parents back home to make sure that all was well with them. We went to the local post office to make the call through our home telephone service. We were proud that we knew how to do this, and that the cost of our call would be minimized.

The lady at the counter in the post office merely glanced up as Nancy entered the telephone booth. She had absolutely no problem making her call. When she hung up we left the building and headed for our car.

As we opened the door to the car, a woman ran up and excitedly asked something in German. I thought that she was asking for the location of a telephone. She didn't seem pleased when I directed her to the door of the post office. After several more attempts, she managed to make us understand that she worked for the post office and that we had forgotten to pay for the local call by which we had reached our home phone service. Pride goeth before the fall.

Conventions

The number of digits you dial to reach a party is different in each country in Europe. The busy tone is different. The dial tone is different. The sound of the phone ringing at the other end is different. For example, in France the ringing sound that comes through the receiver is two short hums. The first time I heard it, I thought it was a busy signal.

If you are calling from a hotel room, you will find that you don't dial 9 to obtain an outside line, you might dial 8. You don't dial 0 to reach an operator, you might dial 12. If you have trouble, read the instructions. They are beside the telephone in a hotel and are posted on the face of the telephone in a phone booth. Often there is an English translation on the phone. If all else fails, ask someone for help.

If you need assistance from the operator, you will be delighted to learn that there is always an English-speaking operator on duty. If you make a call to a place of business, there is almost always an English-speaking person available at the other end of the line. Would it be trite to say that English has become the international "lingua franca?"

Paying for the call

There are two conventions for paying for telephone calls in public telephone booths. One, rapidly dying out, is by coin. The other, and far more common, is by telephone card. You can purchase telephone cards in any small shop that sells newspapers, magazines and tobacco. The cards come in various capacities, so make sure you don't buy an expensive card when you only have a few calls to make. Calls are surprisingly inexpensive. We have made numerous local calls, several intercity calls, and several calls to the U.S. on a single telephone card that cost about $15. Amazing!

The telephone systems that use cards have a small screen on the front of the phone that tells you what to do. Some of them allow you to choose the language of the instruction menu. Before you place the call, they tell you how many units of credit remain on the card. At the end of your call they again tell you how much credit you have left. A local call costs you only one unit from the card. Be careful when placing an intercity or international call. If you use up all of the credit on your card, the telephone will hang up on you without warning.

The telephone curse

Once in Luxembourg I looked for a telephone booth to make a local call. The first one I found operated on a telephone card and not on coins. I kept searching, and every telephone that I found required a telephone card. So, being adaptable, I finally went to a news shop and purchased one. You guessed it. The next telephone booth I found operated only on coins.

Important calls to make

There are a number of important calls that you will probably need to make during your trip. If you want to reserve a hotel room, you will probably do it by telephone. Of course, if you are at another hotel at the time, the local manager (small hotel) or concierge (large hotel) will be happy to do it for you. If you need to change or cancel a room reservation, you will probably do it by telephone, especially if the hotel has recorded your credit card number as a guarantee against the room. Even if you have not been asked for your credit card number, it is basic courtesy to notify a hotel of any change in your plans.

Some hotels disconnect the telephone when a customer checks out. If the telephone in your room doesn't work, contact the desk clerk to have it connected.

The most important call to make is to your airline a day or two before your return flight. It is prudent to verify that the flight schedule has not changed and that your seat reservations are confirmed. Did you remember to write down the local telephone number of your airline before you left home?

One more call is very important. That is the call back home to let your loved ones know that all is well and that you are having a good time. This telephone call will be less expensive if you use a U.S. telephone service. Despite the fact that your home telephone service is quite capable of handling transatlantic calls, the information card that they provide you usually assumes that you are calling from the U.S. An (800) number is conveniently printed on the back of the card. You cannot contact your telephone service by dialing an (800) number in Europe. If you do, you have to dial the U.S. country code first, and then you will be paying for your call twice. You need a different number by which to reach your telephone service from each country that you visit. Make sure that you have obtained the access number for each country before you leave home.

Chapter 17
Safety

Hazards

Will you be in danger in the country that you have chosen to visit? Yes, you will probably be exposed to some danger. No, you will not necessarily be in greater danger than you are at home. Why is that? The reason is that in most of the countries that attract tourists the national economy is significantly enhanced by tourism. For this reason the local authorities make extra efforts to ensure the safety and comfort of visitors. To illustrate my point, you might notice that this is the shortest chapter in the book.

If you visit a developed country in western Europe, you will actually be safer than you are in many places at home. If you visit a relatively undeveloped country or one that is still adjusting to democracy, then you could be in some danger of accidental fallout from local political problems. The best check on possible exposure to danger is look at the website of the U.S. State Department. You can find it at www.travel.state.gov.

In Europe you will see more civil police and more military police on duty than you do at home. This is especially true in large cities and in airports. These are a crossroads of the world. The uniformed officers are there to prevent outsiders from harming the local citizenry, and to prevent them from harming you.

Even so, you would do well to be aware of and to follow some fundamental rules to maximize your personal security. You will find that most of these rules are no different from what you should already be doing at home if you are prudent.

Valuables

Keep your credit cards, travelers checks, passport and the bulk of your cash in a security pouch under your outer clothing. Keep your immediate cash in a shoulder purse or in a buttoned pocket. Be especially conscious of your valuables when in crowded areas. Pickpockets are most frequently found in crowds.

Don't wear expensive jewelry. You are traveling, not participating in a style show. Don't even wear inexpensive jewelry if it happens to look expensive. Once while on the way to O'Hare airport for a trip to Europe, Nancy and I were riding on the "el." The conductor looked at the modest gold chain that Nancy wore around her neck. He commented that if she rode the el long enough, someone would be sure to rip it off.

Don't dress in expensive clothing. It could be damaged by the wear and tear of your travels. Besides, it could mark you as someone who is wealthy.

If you find it handy to carry a guidebook or a map, carry it in a folder, an envelope or a purse. The less you look like a visitor, the less likely you are to attract unwanted attention. This is really a good rule, even though I often don't follow it. That is probably because I need such frequent reference to a map to keep from getting lost.

Walking

When you are walking, avoid areas that might be the haunt of criminals or might expose you to thieves. This includes slums and areas of bawdy nightlife. Avoid going near groups of people who are rowdy or who appear to be high on drugs or alcohol. Avoid going near groups of people whose mode of dress might indicate that they have antisocial tendencies. Keep your eyes open. These unsavory groupings of people do not occur frequently, but they can be anywhere. Once I saw such a group in Geneva, Switzerland, making a lot of noise in a park on the lakeside just in front of a row of luxury hotels.

You should try to stay well clear of demonstrations of any kind. Hostile demonstrations have a way of leading to violence. Happy demonstrations attract pickpockets.

Try to avoid walking in a deserted area, particularly at night. If you disobey this rule, then take care to obey a corollary rule. If you are walking alone in a deserted area, give a wide berth to anyone you see who doesn't appear to be heading for a destination, or who appears to be looking at you too intently.

Try to look "local." I tend to let my hair grow a bit longer than usual before embarking for Europe. You would do well to avoid bright colored clothes and the latest fashion in athletic shoes. Europeans are more conservative in their dress than we are. Don't have a camera hanging around your neck. It brands you immediately as a foreign tourist. Now that I have said that, you probably still look just like an American. Oh, well.

Hotel

If you are staying in a hotel, you might want to consider putting your valuables in the hotel safe. Some hotels even provide safes in the rooms. Make sure that the door to your room is always locked, particularly when you are sleeping and when you are gone.

Leave your hotel key with the desk clerk. It is safer there than on your person. In a small country hotel the keys are hung up on a rack next to the reception desk. This exposes your key to theft, but such theft seems to be extremely rare. That is probably because thieves and strangers are rather obvious in a small facility.

Car

Always lock the door to your car. Don't leave valuables in it. If you have luggage or packages in the car, try to leave them in the trunk where they are not visible. If you have a van, try to cover any personal belongings with something. Yes, I know, this last rule is tough. I only rented a van once, and I was uncomfortable until I had returned it. Of course, nothing was stolen.

Always be courteous in traffic. Europeans seem to be less frustrated by traffic congestion than Americans, but you don't want to attract anyone's hostility. Besides, that person you cut off in traffic, or at whom you yell an obscenity, might be a fellow hostile American.

Welcome to Paris

I was on a business trip a few years before I retired, and had a free weekend in Paris. The plane landed at Orly airport, and I ran to find public transportation to the heart of Paris. I quickly caught a bus that took me to the air terminal just north of the Arch of Triumph.

As I stepped off the bus, my eyes were on the scenery, and my feet were moving quickly so that I wouldn't miss a thing. I did miss something. Within a few steps I had walked into a sidewalk barrier made of piping. The top rail was just at the height of my thighs. I limped for a few days, and wore large bruises for weeks.

Accidents

Remember that small flashlight that I advised you to pack? Always have it at your bedside, and carry it with you at night when you could easily trip over something or fall down a flight of steps. European countries have not experienced the epidemic of personal injury lawsuits that plague our country. For this reason, you will find that stairwells are less well marked. Walkways might have more holes, doorways might be lower, and sidewalk barriers can be at shin height. Again, carry the flashlight at night, and keep your eyes open both day and night. If you are as graceful as I am, you might inflict an injury on yourself.

Chapter 18
Language

Inhibition

In Europe anyone with a high school education speaks at least one language in addition to his native tongue. If a person has a college education, he will be reasonably fluent in at least two languages other than his native tongue. One of these languages is almost certain to be English. However, it is usually the English form of the English language and not American English, unless the person has lived in the U.S. for a period of time.

In the U.S. it is a rare person who can speak another language unless that person is an immigrant or a first generation American. Our colleges and universities have virtually eliminated the language requirement as part of a degree program. Why is this? First of all, our country is about the same size as all of western Europe. It is seldom that an American has the opportunity to speak with someone whose language is other than English. Second, the competition in the job market is intense, and the competition for corporate grants is so fierce that our universities are more occupied with job training than they are with education in the classical sense. How is that for a controversial statement?

Because few Americans are bilingual, they have a built in hesitation about visiting a country that operates in a language other than English. Jack and June experienced that hesitation. We are happy that they did, since it caused them to go on their first European trip with us. They are marvelous travel companions. They have joined us repeatedly, not because of language but because of the enjoyable times we have together.

Pear

Jack has great inhibitions about saying anything in a foreign language. We have noticed, however, that he is finding it easier to read and interpret printed signs. He also seems to be able to identify the main ideas expressed in conversations. But he is still reluctant to speak.

At the end of a trip to France he had decided on a caramelized pear for dessert. He became brave and asked Nancy how to say the word pear. She said "poir." When the waiter came to him to take his dessert order, Jack said "poir." The waiter then asked in French which of two pear desserts he wanted. Jack's response was, "Oh, shit!"

Language adds seasoning

If you know a bit of the language of your target country, it certainly adds a lot to your enjoyment of what you experience. You can understand some (a very small "some") of the finer points of conversation, much of the mannerisms and customs, and almost all of the printed signs. You might even be able to read a menu. For these reasons alone, I recommend that you invest a little time learning some bits of the language that you will be exposed to on your trip.

There is another excellent reason for learning – and using – some basic phrases of a language. You will be greeted with more warmth, courtesy and consideration by the people you meet if you can at least show them that you are trying to learn about them.

Instant experts

Nancy and I were on our first visit to Paris together. We had a nice room at the foot of the Montmartre hill with a great view over the rooftops of Paris. We had only begun to study the language, but greeted the manager in French and used his native language as much as we could.

We went out for dinner and a walk to the top of the hill to visit the Sacre Coeur basilica, and to gaze at the work of the street artists in the Place du Tertre. Upon our return at midnight we found the manager still at his desk. He introduced us to a friend of his who had been waiting all evening to meet us. The friend's daughter had gone to the U.S. to study at New York City College. The man wanted to know if the school was a good one and if she was safe. We innocents from Illinois reassured him on both counts. I hope we were right.

Language is not essential

On the other hand, if you cannot invest the time, or if you are too shy to try to use another language, you can get along quite well without a word of the local tongue. Sign language goes a long way toward establishing understanding. You can point at a map to show where you want to go. A merchant is happy to write out the price of an object if you point at it and make a questioning expression with your face. Many restaurants have English language menus. Even poorly educated Europeans tend to have a smattering of the English language.

You should experience no great language barrier in most of the large cities in Europe. You are, however, quite likely to experience a language barrier in small towns. But in some countries – Belgium, Luxembourg, Portugal, Switzerland – you should find people with basic English skills, even in small villages. In other countries, the small town resident is generally isolated from frequent contact with Anglophiles.

Dictionary of terms

Even if you learn nothing of the local language, you should carry some sort of dictionary of terms with you. A bilingual dictionary is handy, but tends to contain only individual words. Such a dictionary is convenient for the person who has a basic skill in the language. A more useful booklet for the non-speaker is a phrase book. Several companies make pocket-sized phrase books that are organized by topic. There is a page or two for phrases when going through customs (I'd rather not have to talk in customs.) There is a page or two about renting a hotel room. There is a page or two about dining, even though this subject deserves a whole book by itself due to the colorful way in which restaurants describe their dishes. One of the best such publications is a pocket-sized book by Berlitz. Even so, I will offer you a useful alternative in this chapter.

Gelb

We were in the countryside of western Austria and needed gasoline. As the attendant pumped the gas, I noticed that there was a field across the road with a grain that had beautiful golden blossoms. We had seen many such fields all the way from the Frankfurt airport.

I asked the man in my basic German what the name of the golden grain was, using "gelb" the German word for gold. The answer was "gelb." After the question and answer were repeated several times it finally dawned on me that the name of the plant was indeed "gelb." A dictionary verified this brilliant conclusion and told me that it was rapeseed or canola. I like canola better.

The absolute minimum

If you only try to learn a very few phrases, there is a small set of them that will enable you to make a good first impression on people in another country. What sort of impression you make after the first few words is all up to you, and your smile and courtesy. The key phrases are in the vocabulary list on the next page.

Basic Phrases

Do you speak English? _____
Excuse me.   _____
Fine thanks, and you? _____
Good day.   _____
Good evening.   _____
Good morning.   _____
Good night.   _____
Goodby.   _____
Hello.   _____
Help!   _____
How are you?   _____
I don't speak ...   _____
I don't understand. _____
I'd like ...   _____
I'm lost.   _____
My name is ...   _____
No.   _____
Please.   _____
Pleased to meet you. _____
Repeat, please.   _____
Thank you.   _____
Where's the toilet? _____
Yes.   _____
You are welcome. _____

There now, that isn't so bad, is it? Try it, you'll like it. I guarantee that these few phrases will go a long way toward ensuring you a friendly reception. Some people who speak English quite well will pretend that they don't speak it at all, particularly if they have nothing to sell to you. However, if you address them with one or more of the above phrases, they will be more likely to make the attempt to communicate with you. After all, you tried. Besides, their poor English skill is head and shoulders above your French or German or whatever.

Note that all of the English phrases on the list are in bold type. That means that you should learn them by heart so that you can say them at the appropriate time without having to look them up. They are very important to you. The list of words and phrases is three inches by five inches. Make a copy of the page and cut out the box. It will fit nicely in a pocket.

The lace maker

Nancy doesn't like to carry money when we travel, preferring that I carry it for her. Fortunately she has never lost me. One time in Cluny she came running to get money with which to buy some lace. I asked her why she wanted lace. Her answer was that she was talking to the local lace maker whose English was at the same basic level as her French. He was so nice to talk to that she felt obligated to buy something.

On her orders, I stayed at a distance in order not to interfere with the conversation. They were waving their arms violently. If it hadn't been for the smiles on their faces, I would have thought they were fighting. Yes, she bought some lace.

Pocket phrase book

Despite the fact that a number of companies publish convenient phrase books, I am offering you a simplified one here. I hope that you find it to be useful. It consists of a series of three by five cards similar to the one on the previous page. You can carry them in a pocket when you go to a restaurant or obtain a room at a hotel. Besides, if you take the time to fill in the blanks on the cards, then you will have progressed a long way toward learning more than the bare minimum of your target language.

On the remaining vocabulary lists in this chapter the English phrases are either in bold, italic, or normal type. Memorize the ones in bold type. They are the most important to have on the tip of your tongue. Learn the ones in italics so that you can recognize them when you see them or hear them. You will need to react to some of them quickly. This includes a number of road signs. Gain a bit of familiarity with the ones in normal type. These include such words as those for types of buildings and types of foods. Usually you will have adequate time to look up these words in your three by five cards when you need them.

Do these lists of words and phrases really help? I can assure you that they do. I had never studied the Portuguese language. As I prepared for our first trip to Portugal I filled out a set of these cards. They worked marvelously. No, I was not a Portuguese linguist. Yes, I did get along quite well, even with people who spoke no English. Of course, I didn't discuss anything like philosophy or politics.

Make an investment

Certainly you have noticed that none of these vocabulary lists includes a translation. The only words are English. This is for two good reasons. A set of cards in each European language would make this book too large. Besides, as you look up the words in German, or French, or whatever, you are making an investment in your vocabulary. It is your first step toward learning the important words and phrases.

The perils of English English

Winston Churchill once remarked that our two countries were doomed to be forever separated by a common language. True. I was on a train in Japan when a college student boarded the car and sat beside me. In very precise and polite English he asked if he might have intercourse with me. Ever have a choking fit?

Buildings

bakery _____
bank _____
building _____
castle _____
cathedral _____
church _____
city hall _____
concert hall _____
fort _____
gas station _____
grocery _____
hotel _____
information _____
museum _____
news stand _____
night club _____
opera _____
palace _____
pharmacy _____
police station _____
post office _____
restaurant _____
supermarket _____

Calendar

Sunday _____
Monday _____
Tuesday _____
Wednesday _____
Thursday _____
Friday _____
Saturday _____
January _____
February _____
March _____
April _____
May _____
June _____
July _____
August _____
September _____
October _____
November _____
December _____

_____
_____
_____
_____

Clothing

bathrobe
belt
bra
coat
dress
hat
jacket
panties
raincoat
scarf
shirt
shoes
skirt
slip
slippers
stockings
suit
sweater
tie
trousers
umbrella
underclothes

Colors

beige
black
blue
brown
color
copper
dark
gold
gray
green
light
orange
pink
purple
red
silver
violet
white
yellow

Customs

customs
declaration
I'm going to ...
I'm on vacation
I'm on business
liquor
luggage
nothing to declare
passport
perfume
suitcase
tobacco

Directions

back _____
direction _____
down _____
east _____
facing _____
far _____
fast _____
here _____
I'm lost _____
in the center _____
left _____
near _____
next to _____
north _____
right _____
slow _____
south _____
straight ahead _____
street _____
toward _____
up _____
west _____
where is ... _____

Drinks

aperitif
bottle
coffee
cream
cup
dark beer
draft beer
espresso
glass
ice
juice
milk
red wine
soda
tea
water w/o gas
water with gas
whiskey
white wine

Family

ancestor _____
aunt _____
brother _____
daughter _____
family _____
father _____
grandfather _____
grandmother _____
great-grandfather _____
great-grandmother _____
I am an American _____
He died _____
He was born _____
mother _____
my family _____
niece _____
nephew _____
toots _____
sister _____
she was born _____
son _____
uncle _____
_____

Foods

bread
boiled
butter
cereal
cheese
custard
egg
fried
ice cream
jam
ketchup
mustard
pastry
pepper
rice
roll
salad
salt
soup
sugar
toast
vinegar
yogurt

Fruit

apple
avocado
blueberry
cherry
coconut
grape
grapefruit
lemon
lime
melon
olive
orange
peach
pear
pineapple
plum
raisin
raspberry
rhubarb
strawberry
tangerine

Genealogy

A copy, please _____
archives _____
birth certificate _____
book _____
bookstore _____
city hall _____
clerk _____
death certificate _____
discharge _____
document _____
genealogist _____
heraldry _____
librarian _____
library _____
marriage certificate _____
mayor _____
museum _____
rectory _____
registry _____
secretary _____
They were married _____
When? _____
_____

Jewelry

bracelet
brooch
chain
crystal
diamond
earring
engraving
gold
jewel
jewelry
medal
medallion
necklace
pendant
pewter
pin
ring
ruby
silver
watch

Lodging

bed and breakfast _____
concierge _____
double bed _____
double room _____
elevator _____
garage _____
ground floor _____
hotel _____
I have a reservation. _____
key _____
May I see the room? _____
one night _____
room with bath _____
shower _____
single room _____
soap _____
staircase _____
television _____
toilet _____
toilet paper _____
towel _____
twin beds _____
with breakfast _____

Meals

appetizer _____
Bill, please. _____
breakfast _____
daily special _____
delicious _____
dessert _____
dinner _____
entree _____
fast food _____
fixed price _____
fork _____
Is a tip included? _____
knife _____
lunch _____
menu _____
napkin _____
plate _____
restaurant _____
snack _____
spoon _____
Waiter! _____
Waitress! _____
wine menu _____

Meat

bacon
beef
chicken
clams
cutlet
duck
fish
flounder
ham
lamb
medium
mussels
pork
rare
salmon
sausage
shrimp
steak
trout
tuna
turkey
veal
well done

Money

ATM machine
bank
Change, please.
Coins, please.
credit card
Do you accept ...
I want to exchange ...
personal check
travelers check

Numbers - small

0
1
2
3
4
5
6
7
8
9
10
11
12
13
14
15
16
17
18
19
20
21
22

Numbers - large

30 _____
40 _____
50 _____
60 _____
70 _____
80 _____
90 _____
100 _____
101 _____
200 _____
500 _____
1000 _____
2000 _____
20,000 _____
200,000 _____
1,000,000 _____
2,000,000 _____

_____
_____
_____
_____
_____
_____

Shopping

bargain
bigger
cheaper
credit card
Do you have ...?
entrance
exit
expensive
Help me, please.
How much is it?
I'll take it.
I'm just looking.
I'm looking for ...
less
more
sale
smaller
that
this
VAT
VAT receipt, please.
Write it, please.

Signs

CLOSED _____
DANGER _____
DETOUR _____
DIESEL FUEL _____
GASOLINE _____
INFORMATION _____
MEN _____
NO ADMITTANCE _____
NO PARKING _____
NO SMOKING _____
NO TRESPASSING _____
ONE WAY _____
OPEN _____
PARKING _____
PEDESTRIAN ZONE _____
PRIVATE _____
REST STOP _____
SERVICE STATION _____
SLOW _____
TOILET _____
TOLL BOOTH _____
VACANCY _____
WOMEN _____

Time

date
day
hour
in the afternoon
in the evening
in the morning
in the night
It's 10:00
It's 10:15
It's 10:30
It's 10:45
It's 10:50
month
now
today
tomorrow
week
year
yesterday
What time is it?

Transportation

airplane _____
airport _____
arrivals _____
baggage claim _____
bus _____
bus stop _____
car rental _____
entrance _____
exit _____
first class _____
non-smoking _____
one way _____
round trip _____
second class _____
sleeper _____
smoking _____
station _____
subway _____
taxi _____
ticket _____
train _____
transfer _____
trolley _____

Vegetables

artichoke
asparagus
beans
broccoli
cabbage
cauliflower
celery
corn
endive
garlic
green beans
lettuce
mushrooms
onion
parsley
peas
pepper
potato
radish
sauerkraut
squash
tomato

Phonics

Of course, all languages do not pronounce all letters of the alphabet the same way. Some languages, like Spanish, are missing some of the 26 letters that we are accustomed to. Some languages, like French, add accents to letters as in é, è, and ê. Some languages, such as Russian, have a totally different alphabet, using characters such as д, and ж. Some languages, such as Arabic, not only use strange looking characters such as ۳ and ث, but they write from right to left.

If you are going to be able to speak or read a bit of the language, you will have to be able to pronounce the words in a somewhat similar fashion to that of a native speaker. However, unless you are unusually talented, you will speak with a heavy accent. Even if you don't try to speak in the language, you will want to be able to read signs and menus. It is easier to do so if you can sound out the words.

For this reason, I have added one more reminder card for you to use to write the phonics of your target language. As an example, I have added a sample card of the Portuguese language. I used it on the trip to Portugal and found it to be a great asset. If you compare this example to the Berlitz phrase book, you will find out that I have grossly simplified the pronunciation rules. The idea is to be reasonably understandable, not to become fluent. If you want to become fluent in a language, then nothing beats a school with a native teacher, followed by months in the country where the language is spoken.

On a trip to Russia, Nancy learned to sound out the 33 characters of the Cyrillic alphabet. She was definitely able to read signs. It proved to be of great value to her on the subway. Besides, as she read the signs on stores, she found out that many of the words were cognates, derived from English, and thus understandable. It added greatly to her enjoyment of the visit.

Oh yes, where do you get the phonics equivalents? I have found two fine sources. One is the Berlitz phrase book. The other is a CD audio tape for language study. The first gives you the equivalent sound in print. The second lets you hear how it really sounds from the mouth of a native speaker. Watch the vowels carefully. They are the sounds that really show up your foreign accent and make you difficult to understand.

As long as you are going to listen to a bit of a language CD or audio tape, listen to it repeatedly. This will give you a significant advantage in recognizing some of the speech patterns of your target language. It will help you to understand native speakers. Remember, your purpose in listening to the recording repeatedly is not to gain fluency, but to be able to recognize words as you hear them. If you don't do this, a sentence spoken by a native will probably just sound like a string of sounds without any meaningful breaks.

Phonics - Portuguese

char(s)	sound	char(s)	sound
ce	say	è	ay
ci	see	i	ih
ca	kah	o	oa
co	ko	ô	oh
cu	koo	ou	oh
ç	s	u	oo
ch	sh	em	eng
ge	zhay	en	eng
gi	zhee	âo	awm
ga	gah	ti	chi
go	go	te	che
gu	goo	ho	yo
h	(silent)	final s	sh
j	zh		
lh	ly		
nh	ny		
q	k		
r	(trilled)		
x	sh		
a	ah		
e	eh		
é	eh		

Phonics
Portuguese

char(s)	sound	char(s)	sound

Chapter 19
Returning Home

Preparation

What preparation is necessary to return home? Isn't it just a matter of putting things back in the suitcases, boarding the plane, and flying home? Nope, there is more to it than that, especially if you want to end your trip on an up-note. A lot of things can go wrong if you don't prepare for your return. Besides, it really doesn't take a lot of effort to ensure a happy trip home.

Flight confirmation

First of all you would do well to confirm your flight time and your seat reservations a day or two before you are scheduled to return. Remember that phone number you obtained before you left home so that you could call the office of your airline in the country from which you will be departing? Don't worry about language. The person who answers the telephone will be fluent in English. One time in France when I checked on a return flight I addressed the airline clerk in French. He immediately responded in English and told me that if I preferred to speak English he would do so. He was Irish. So much for my French accent.

If you are tempted for a bump, this same telephone call can give you a clue or two as to the possibility. After all, a bump will give you a travel voucher of $700 or more in value, plus another day in Europe with your room and meals paid for. Such a deal! The person who confirms your flight will be pleased to tell you how fully booked your flight is.

Packing

If you are like us, you will have accumulated a few, or more than a few, treasures to take home with you. They will need to be packed with care. Some are breakable. Some will set off the x-ray machine if they are in carry-on luggage, causing you to have to open the bag to prove that you aren't carrying a bomb or other illegal device. This is always a delay and an irritation. Besides, you can well have difficulty putting everything back into the opened bag.

Although we try to avoid having any check-in luggage on the flight to Europe, we sometimes find it convenient to check one of the stewardess-type suitcases on the way home. It saves pulling it through airports. Besides, there is nothing in it that we will need right away when we arrive home. If the bag is misrouted we can afford to wait for it to be found and returned to us. We put into this bag anything that is bulky or heavy, and anything that is unbreakable.

There are a few things that you should move from the suitcase to the purse or briefcase. You will need them when you arrive home. They are the purse of U.S. coins and your house and car keys. You can move a few things in the other direction, things like maps, guidebooks, and the power converter.

Watch at the carousel upon arrival to see the tears of people who have packed bottles of expensive liquor in check-in luggage. You should also see the tears when they arrive home and open the bag to see what the alcohol has done to the other contents. I remember a French friend who packed several bottles of a heavy, sweet liqueur in his check-in suitcase. He had also packed a green folder with a business report. The bottles broke and soaked everything. The green folder dissolved and ran over all of the clothes. No report. Big laundry bill.

If you hope to get a bump you will want to put overnight things in one of your small carry-on bags. Your check-in luggage will already be on its way home on your scheduled flight. You can't use anything from it. Besides, even if you don't check anything, you don't want to have to unpack everything all over again for just a single extra night in a hotel. If you have a connecting flight at home, you might get another chance for a bump, or you might miss the flight, or it might be canceled. In any of these cases you will be happy to have your overnight things in a small bag.

We find it convenient to put breakable things into a small carry-on bag. If we have more than the bag can hold, we put the larger and heavier things into one of the stewardess-style suitcases and pack it with soiled clothing. Oh yes, we first place that soiled clothing into some of the plastic bags that we brought with us. Did you remember the ties for those bags?

If we still have too much luggage, we put all of the dirty clothes into the large nylon bag that we packed in the bottom of a suitcase when we left home. We check in this bag.

As you pack all of those things that you bought, make a list of them and note the approximate dollar value of each. If you bought anything with a value of $100 or more, put the receipt with the list and place it in your pocket or in a small piece of carry-on luggage. You will want to refer to it during the flight when you make out the declaration form for customs. Also write on the list the approximate value of any gifts that you received.

Most international airlines are finding themselves tightly strapped for storage space in the airplane cabins. You are likely to see a sign at the check-in desk stating that the limit for carry-on luggage is one bag. Best to have checked this out when you made that phone call to confirm your flight. Usually, despite the sign, you will be told that two bags are acceptable as long as one of them is "small," like a large purse or a briefcase. One goes in the overhead and the other, smaller bag goes under the seat in front of you.

The pétanque bombs

A popular game in France is called boules or pétanque. It is somewhat similar to the Italian bocci ball. In pétanque the balls are about the size of a softball and are made of stainless steel, since the game is often played on gravel parking lots.

We were bringing a pétanque set home in our carry-on luggage when we checked in for our flight from Orly airport in Paris. The balls showed up on the x-ray machine as eight large black circles. Naturally I was asked to open the bag. The clerk chuckled, but said he would keep the balls. He stated that they would be returned to me upon our arrival at home. I wondered why, but then realized that the balls had machined grooves on their surface. The grooves could disguise a joint in a hollow ball where nasty substances could be concealed.

Just before the flight was to leave, my name was called. The clerk informed me that they had inspected the balls and I could have them back. I was disappointed. Now I had to carry the load myself.

Returning the car

When you return the car at the airport on the last day, you will want to do so earlier in the day than when you picked it up. Otherwise you might have to pay for an extra day. This is the same principle as for most U.S. rentals. You will also want to fill the tank. There will be at least one gas station near the airport. Did you remember to locate where you picked up the car?

If you forgot where to turn in the car, and if you are in a hurry, park it in any lot. Then make a written note of where it is parked, and give the note to the agent to whom you return the papers. The check-in procedure is usually as simple and as efficient as in the U.S.

Check-in

The airlines want you to check in for your flight at least two hours in advance. During the last hour or so before your flight the lines for check-in can become incredibly long. You go through a brief interview where you are asked to confirm that your bags don't contain anything that might jeopardize anyone. Then you go through the baggage check-in station, whether you are checking luggage or not. Next you go for a long walk to the international portion of the terminal. Then you go through the passport check. Then you go for another long walk to your gate. Remember to confirm your arrival with the clerk at that gate too. If you make it to this last station at least ten minutes before your scheduled departure time, the airline is responsible to provide you a seat or a bump. Miss that ten-minute window, and you could be out of luck.

We tend to arrive at the airport about three hours before our scheduled departure. The flight home usually leaves shortly after noon. This doesn't leave enough of the morning to do any sightseeing anyway. One might as wait at the airport as at the hotel. Besides, the earlier we arrive, the higher we are on the list for a bump. And we avoid standing in long, slow lines when the check-in crunch comes. While others are grumbling, we are having a coffee and reading the newspaper. We also have time to browse the airport shops.

Remember the old adage. "If you aren't in a hurry, take a plane."

Left luggage

Anyone who has flown knows that the airports do not like to see a piece of luggage sitting around unattended, since it might contain a bomb. I once set a briefcase down outside a book shop in the airport at Glasgow while I browsed the shelves. A huge policeman came by and informed me in no uncertain terms that, "We don't do that."

Another time, when I approached the passport check in Geneva, the line had grown long and wasn't moving. I could see through the glass doors that there were a number of police inside the international portion of the terminal. They had placed yellow tape lines in a large square around a suitcase that was sitting unattended in the middle of the floor. Just then a young man came by and asked, "What are they doing with my suitcase?" He was not given a friendly reception by the police.

Foreign currency

Unless you are a very careful planner or are very lucky, you will wind up at the airport with some quantity of money from the country or countries that you have visited. What to do with it?

You can bring it home with you. I usually do this if the amount is less than $100 and if I plan to visit the country again within a few years. However, with the imminent advent of the euro in the European Economic Community I now have a limited number of years to exchange this money for euros.

You can exchange paper money for dollars. If you do this, you will find the exchange rate a bit unfavorable and to the advantage of the money exchange desk in the airport.

What do you do with the coins? The United Nations has begun to display collection boxes in international terminals for you to use to dispose of unneeded and unexchangeable coins. They are used to support charitable work. A neat idea.

You can spend the surplus foreign currency. You can buy coffee, magazines or books, candy, or a great variety of items that are displayed in little shops in the international terminal. Talk about impulse buying!

You can buy things in the duty-free shop. This is not a bad idea. Some of the things are truly a bargain. Besides, the clerk will take all of your foreign money of whatever country, and will then tell you how many dollars you owe in addition. Watch out though. If you have to break a travelers check to make up the difference, the change you get will be in the currency of that country. Catch 22! Try using a charge card to make up the difference. Or use some of those greenbacks you brought with you from home. Don't tell me you packed them in the bottom of the suitcase that you checked.

Did you also remember to dig out the U.S. coins that you brought with you? You might need them when you land. They are handy for phone calls or hamburgers. Speaking of hamburgers, did you experience withdrawal while in Europe?

The flight

Like on the flight to Europe, the stewards and stewardesses visit you frequently in order to distract you so that the trip seems shorter. You will land at home the same afternoon, but your day will have been seven hours longer than normal. A nap or two can be a great help to enable you to survive until you reach your own bed. Even though the flight is during daylight hours, we find that we sleep better than we did on the first flight. I think the reason is fatigue. On our last trip neither Nancy nor I saw one minute of the movie. It was advertised as an excellent film, but we didn't feel that we had missed anything important.

One of the visits by the airplane crew is for the distribution of customs declaration forms. You only need to fill out one form per family. Put the completed form in the same place where you keep your passports and plane tickets.

Arrival

When you arrive at the airport in the U.S., your first stop will be at the passport check. The lines will be long, especially if other airplanes have landed just before yours. This often seems to be the case. If you hate lines, head immediately for the one farthest away from where you entered the room. It is usually the shortest. Make sure that it is the line for U.S. citizens and not one for foreigners or for airline crews and diplomats. The clerk will want to see the customs declaration form and the passports of all the people in your family who are traveling together. He will stamp your passports and then return them to you together with the customs declaration form.

Your second stop is at the carousel to pick up your check-in luggage. Usually you will arrive there before the luggage does. If you have no check-in luggage, you can go directly to the customs clerk at the exit from the room with the luggage carousel. This clerk will take your declaration form. If there is no irregularity, and if you have an honest face, you will be directed to the exit. If you are over any import limit or look suspicious, you will be directed to a line where you will be questioned, some of your luggage might be opened and inspected, some of your money might be paid in duty, some of your purchases might be confiscated, and some of your temper might be frayed. Best to be legal and look honest. If you are stopped, don't panic or feel insulted. The customs people stop a small percentage of people at random. It has happened to me. They will be polite and will release you promptly.

Your last stop, if you are making a connecting flight, is to check in your luggage one last time. Most airports have a desk just outside the customs area to make this last process as convenient as possible.

Just one bottle

In 1990 Ed was visiting in Belgium between Christmas and New Year's Day. When he and April had lived there, their favorite beverage was called Geuze, something between beer and wine, bottled by the Bellevue Brewery. While shopping, he stumbled upon a five-liter bottle that was made by the brewery as a Christmas promotion. He tells me he bought it – for April of course.

To keep it from breaking on the way home, he put it in his carry-on bag wrapped in towels. When he reached customs at home, it dawned on him that he was over his alcohol limit. What to do? When the agent asked if he had alcohol to declare, he said, "Just one bottle." He didn't add that it was 28 inches tall and two feet around. The empty bottle still sits in a prominent place in his home.

Home at last!

You have reached your local airport. How do you get home? We have developed a system that works well for us. Since we might get a bump, and since flights are not always on schedule, we don't ask anyone to meet us at the airport. Instead, we carry the key to our car and give another key to good friends. One friend drives to the airport in our car the morning before we are scheduled to arrive. The other friend drives another car and takes the first person home after our car has been left in a preselected location. That way we have transportation when we arrive, whenever we arrive, and nobody has to wait for us.

Now you are in your own house, but tired, very tired. We have another system for this. We read the mail. It keeps us awake and active. We catch up on the news. And we allow our adrenaline to settle down to the point where we can truly get a good night's sleep. One good night's sleep is usually enough to overcome most of the jet lag syndrome. When are you over jet lag? When your bodily functions operate at the same time of day as they did before you left home in the first place. Need I be more specific?

Chapter 20
Do's and Don't's

Introduction

This chapter contains a number of items that seem worth bringing to your attention, but which don't fit easily in any of the other chapters. Other items were touched on briefly elsewhere in the book, but deserve to be highlighted in some way. I hope that you enjoy them, and profit from them.

Shutdown

When you leave home your house will be unattended for a few weeks unless you have made plans for a house-sitter. There are a few things that you can do to minimize problems and expenses.
- Do consider shutting off the water. Twice we have returned home to find a plumbing problem. In each case we were fortunate that the problem occurred the day before we arrived. If it had happened the day after we left, the repair costs could have been high.
- Do shut off, better yet unplug, major electronic devices such as TV's, stereos and computers. Lightening does bad things to delicate circuitry.

Looking American

Europeans seem to have an uncanny ability to spot an American. In Luxembourg this can be an advantage, since the typical Luxembourger is quite aware of the sacrifice that American troops made in and for their country during the Battle of the Bulge in WWII. In some other countries, looking like an American can brand you as someone to take advantage of. For example, I have been in an Italian restaurant that makes it a practice of serving Americans cheap wine while charging for first class wine. It is an easy way to make an extra profit from a customer who doesn't know the customs or the language. Assuming that you would rather not be immediately obvious as an American and as a tourist, I offer you the following thoughts.

- Don't use hand signals when you talk. They can mean quite different things in different countries. Some of the meanings are obscene. For example, making a circle with thumb and forefinger indicates approval in the U.S. In Italy it means the same obscenity as lifting the middle finger does in the U.S.
- Don't say "hi" or wave at people. Don't give a big smile to strangers that you pass on the street. It immediately brands you as an American. If you want to be friendly, and you should be, it is better to smile slightly (no teeth) and nod or say hello in the local language.
- Don't speak in a loud voice. Most Europeans are soft-spoken and generally undemonstrative in public. This characteristic is missing in many football (soccer) fans, especially English fans.

Why can't you speak English?

Ed was at a streetcar stop in Woluwe, a suburb of Brussels. A man asked him in French how to get to the train station. Ed's French was adequate for basic necessities, but was definitely not fluent. He tried for fifteen minutes to explain to the man how to get to the station, but the message just didn't seem to get across. Finally, the man muttered in English: "I wish you spoke bleedin' English." Obviously, both men were embarrassed. The needed directions were then quickly given and followed.

Communications

Expect some difficulty in communicating with people. This even happens in England. They have many expressions that are different from the ones we use. This problem is compounded, of course, when you are in a country where a different language is used.

- Do be careful if you are in the habit of showing fingers to emphasize a number from one to three. If you say "one" beer and hold up your index finger, you might be delivered two beers. The Europeans use the thumb to indicate one. They use the thumb and index finger to indicate two, and the thumb and next two fingers to indicate three. Did you ever hear the story of the man who ordered a dry martini in Germany and was delivered three?
- Don't blame a misunderstanding on the poor moral character of the people in another country. Most people are decent and honest. If a misunderstanding costs you inconvenience or money, it might be just that – a misunderstanding.
- Don't take sides. In some countries, such as in Belgium and Switzerland, people in different areas speak different languages. In these specific countries, and in some others many people dislike their fellow citizens who speak another tongue. A French-speaking Swiss might point at another person and tell you with a sneer, "After all, he is Swiss German." Your best response is to give a slight, knowing smile and say nothing.
- Don't say "yes" if someone says something that you don't understand. It is safer and more polite to admit that you did not understand. Better yet, say it in the local language.
- Do be careful when you write or read a date. We Americans are the only ones in the world who write July 6, 1998 as 7/6/98. Most of the rest of the world would write the date as 6.7.98 or better, 6.7.1998. Note the sequence of day before month. You would be better to write a date as the Europeans do it, with the periods, or write it as 6July1998 or as July 6, 1998. You don't want to miss your flight home, do you? In Scandinavian countries the date is written as year, then month, then day.

- Do be careful when you state a time of day. European transportation tends to operate on what we would call the military clock. This is a 24-hour clock where 6 p.m. is written or spoken as 18:00. Everybody understands 18:00 as 6:00 p.m., transportation or not.
- Don't judge a country by a border town. For some subtle sociological reason that eludes me, the towns at the border crossings tend not to show either country in the best of lights. They seem to be a bit seamy, or a whole lot seamy, around the edges. If your first entry into a country is disappointing, wait until you are deeper into the country before beginning to judge it.

The irate Rhine maiden

We were touring the castles along the Rhine in Germany. Although traffic signs in Europe are usually simple and clear, private signs can be less communicative. We saw a sign pointing toward a castle we had been seeking. The sign was not easy to see, and was covered with writing.

By the time we had pulled the rear of the car off the highway, we were already passing the sign. We progressed up a winding gravel road. Suddenly a lady appeared ahead of us. In a loud and angry voice she informed us that we were driving on a footpath and should leave it promptly. The only way out was to go back. As we passed the sign more slowly on our return, we could see hidden in the lengthy text the magic word "Fußweg" or footpath. Oh well.

Dogs

Europeans love their dogs. They also take their dogs with them to places where you would take your children. Don't let it put you off. Remember that this is their country, not yours.
- Do watch your step on the sidewalks and when crossing the street. The pooper-scooper concept has not taken hold yet. This is particularly true in Belgium where the sidewalks are badly littered. In Germany and France the dog owner will try, but not always succeed, to place his dog in the gutter or next to a tree at the proper moment.

- Don't be surprised to see a dog in a restaurant with its owners. I have seen a customer's dog beside his chair in French restaurants. I have seen the restaurant owner's dog under a table in a Luxembourg restaurant. I have seen a customer's dog sitting on a chair and eating from a bowl on the table in a Belgian restaurant. Most amazing of all, I have seen a man going up the main aisle at a Catholic Mass for Communion, with his little dog in his arm.

Solicitations

On occasion you might be approached on the street by someone offering to buy or sell something. There are rare occasions when this could be to your advantage. There are more frequent occasions when the prudent thing to do is to say "no, thank you" politely, and walk away.
- Don't buy anything expensive from a street merchant, even if the price is low and the item has a well-known brand name. It is probably a fake, and could cause you a problem at a customs check.
- Don't buy anything from someone on the street who doesn't have his merchandise displayed. The item is probably stolen property.
- Don't exchange dollars for local currency with anyone on the street. At best you might find that the local currency being offered is counterfeit. At worst you are in danger of arrest for dealing in the black market. If you can afford to travel, you can afford to accept the market rate of exchange from reputable dealers.
- Do consider selling your jeans or shoes or other peculiarly American items if approached on the street, particularly if you are a young person who is traveling on a shoestring. Although you are dealing in the black market, it is really a sort of gray market that won't put you in danger. That is, if you aren't walking in your underclothes after having sold your jeans.
- Do be careful about bartering for a bargain. You might insult the merchant. While barter is a way of life in the Orient and in the Near East, it generally doesn't work in most places in

western Europe. Of course, a merchant might offer you an instant discount if you suggest that the price of an item is a bit higher than you are prepared to pay. This is especially true when you are buying a craft item from the person who made it. It doesn't hurt if you have already been highly complimentary about the quality of the workmanship. If you are paying a large amount for the item and ask for a receipt and an application for recovery of VAT (value added tax,) the craftsman might offer you a price discount instead. Real artists hate paperwork.
- Do accept recommendations from local people about places to shop for specific items, especially if you have asked for the recommendation. Have a care, however, if the recommendation is for one specific store, and if you haven't asked for it. You just might have encountered a shill who is setting you up for being overcharged while he gets a finder fee.
- Don't take "free" offers unless you are ready to pay for them. For example, if someone voluntarily directs you to a parking place, it might be his way of earning some money in the form of tips.
- Do be polite to someone who strikes up a conversation with you. The person might just be friendly like Stammtisch Willi in Chapter 11.

The hurried cab hustler

We had arrived in Paris for the first time, by train from Brussels. As we left the station, we lined up for a cab. The line was very long, and moved ahead very slowly.

A man came up and offered to find us a cab at what seemed a low cost. I agreed. The man picked up two of our bags and dashed off. As Nancy and I hurried after him, she asked what price he had quoted. I told her. Being a bookkeeper where I am only a mathematician, she asked if I knew how many dollars that was. I did a high speed calculation and shouted "STOP!" The man dropped the suitcases so suddenly that they skidded down the street as he hurried off after another sucker. We took the subway.

Building conventions

The population is quite a bit denser in Europe than it is in our country. They also have many more centuries of history than we do here. This makes for some architectural features that might be a surprise, sometimes a painful surprise. You will have ample opportunity to injure yourself on cobblestone streets, uneven stairs, and low doorways.

- Do watch your step when walking in a medieval area. The cobblestone streets can cause you to trip or to turn an ankle.
- Do watch your head when going through doorways in medieval buildings. People were a lot shorter in the old days.
- Don't expect large cars or large hotel rooms. They are adequate for their purpose in Europe, but are usually quite a bit smaller than their American counterparts. If you must have a large size, you will pay for it disproportionately.
- Don't expect doors on public buildings to open outwards. They usually open inwards. They never had a Chicago Theater fire in Europe. It was that fire, where people died in a crush trying to leave through an inward-opening door, that led to laws in our country requiring doors in public buildings to open outward.
- Do pause for a moment if the key doesn't seem to work when you are trying to lock a door. On some doors you have to lift the door handle as you turn the key.

Americain flambé

Jacques and Michèle, who live on the side of a mountain in the Isère river valley in the Alps, had invited us to the wedding of their daughter. The reception was in an old chateau. People were seated at tables of eight, with candelabra in the middle. The effect was charming.

I was standing in a doorway chatting with some people when others came to the door. I backed up next to a table to let them by, not noticing that on this particular table the candelabrum had not been centered. I felt a sudden warmth at the same time as someone pointed out that the back of my suit coat was on fire. Americain flambé.

Food and drink

The hardest thing in the world to translate is a menu. Restaurants seem to think that the more colorful the language, the more desirable the dish. On the contrary, the more colorful the language, the less descriptive it is. I have eaten in restaurants with people whose native language is the same as that of the restauranteur. They find it necessary to ask for detailed descriptions. For example, consider what you might expect to find at home in a "chef's salad" or "nachos grande" or "meatloaf." You pays your money and you takes your chances.

- Do order your meat more thoroughly done than you would at home. Well-done meat is not popular in Europe. The result is that it will usually come to you pinker or even redder than you might have expected. Of course, in case of a real shocker, you can send it back for a bit more heat.
- Do flex with menu surprises. If a dish doesn't turn out to be what you expected, try it. You just might like it. Or trade it with the "garbage can" in your group.
- Do expect the coffee to be a lot stronger than you are accustomed to at home. If you have difficulty with it, you might ask for coffee with milk. It is hot milk. Or you might add sugar. Or both.
- Don't just order coffee if you don't like espresso. Order a large coffee. If you do like espresso, and if that is what you are served, and if it is extremely strong, add a bit of sugar or ask for a bit of lemon peel to take away the bitterness. Frankly, I love it.

I refuse

I was on a business trip to Paris. A work associate was traveling with me. He was not a traveler, and thought that the only food fit for human consumption was beef and potatoes. Obviously he was in culture shock in Paris. A French friend had invited us to dinner at a fancy restaurant on the Left Bank. I asked him to help my associate with his meal order.

The waiter came. My friend asked what my associate wanted to eat, and translated a few menu items. The answer was, "steak." He translated to French for the waiter, who asked how Monsieur would like the steak done. My friend translated that question. The answer was, "very well done." Before he could translate that, the waiter said with a sneer and in perfect English, "I refuse."

That's it

Well, that's it. The accumulated experiences, and wisdom, and misadventures, and fun, and foolishness of six couples. I sincerely hope that it proves to be of value to you.

Please don't think that you have to take all of the advice in this book in order to have an enjoyable trip in Europe. Use what you like; reject what you don't like. Remember that we don't follow all of our own advice.

One final reminder. The more you learn about the culture and history of the places you visit, the more you will enjoy the visit. I find that at the end of each trip I am motivated to learn more about the places we have been. Knowledge makes for better experiences. Good experiences encourage the search for more knowledge.

Have a great trip!